THE EASY GUITAR SOURCEBOOK

50 GUITAR GREATS

THE GOLD EDITION

KU-593-645

Exclusive Distributors:
Music Sales Limited
8/9 Frith Street, London W1V 5TZ, England.
Music Sales Pty Limited
120 Rothschild Avenue, Rosebery, NSW 2018, Australia.

Order No. AM936848
ISBN 0-7119-5728-2
This book © Copyright 1996 by Wise Publications

Unauthorised reproduction of any part of this publication by any
means including photocopying is an infringement of copyright.

Compiled by Peter Evans
Book design by Pearce Marchbank, Studio Twenty
Computer layout by Ben May
Music arranged and processed by Paul Lawley

Printed in the United Kingdom by
Redwood Books, Trowbridge, Wiltshire

Your Guarantee of Quality
As publishers, we strive to produce every book to the highest commercial standards.
This book has been carefully designed to minimise awkward page turns and to make playing
from it a real pleasure. Particular care has been given to specifying acid-free, neutral-sized paper
made from pulps which have not been elemental chlorine bleached. This pulp is from farmed
sustainable forests and was produced with special regard for the environment.
Throughout, the printing and binding have been planned to ensure a sturdy, attractive
publication which should give years of enjoyment. If your copy fails to meet our high
standards, please inform us and we will gladly replace it.

Music Sales' complete catalogue describes thousands of titles and
is available in full colour sections by subject, direct from Music Sales Limited.
Please state your areas of interest and send a cheque/postal order for £1.50 for postage to
Music Sales Limited, Newmarket Road, Bury St.Edmunds, Suffolk IP33 3YB.

Visit the Internet Music Shop at http://www.musicsales.co.uk

This publication is not authorised for sale in
the United States of America and/or Canada

Wise Publications
London/New York/Paris/Sydney/Copenhagen/Madrid

ALL THAT SHE WANTS

Words & Music by Buddha & Joker

© Copyright 1992 Megasong Publishing, Sweden.
PolyGram Music Publishing Limited, 47 British Grove, London W4.
All Rights Reserved. International Copyright Secured.

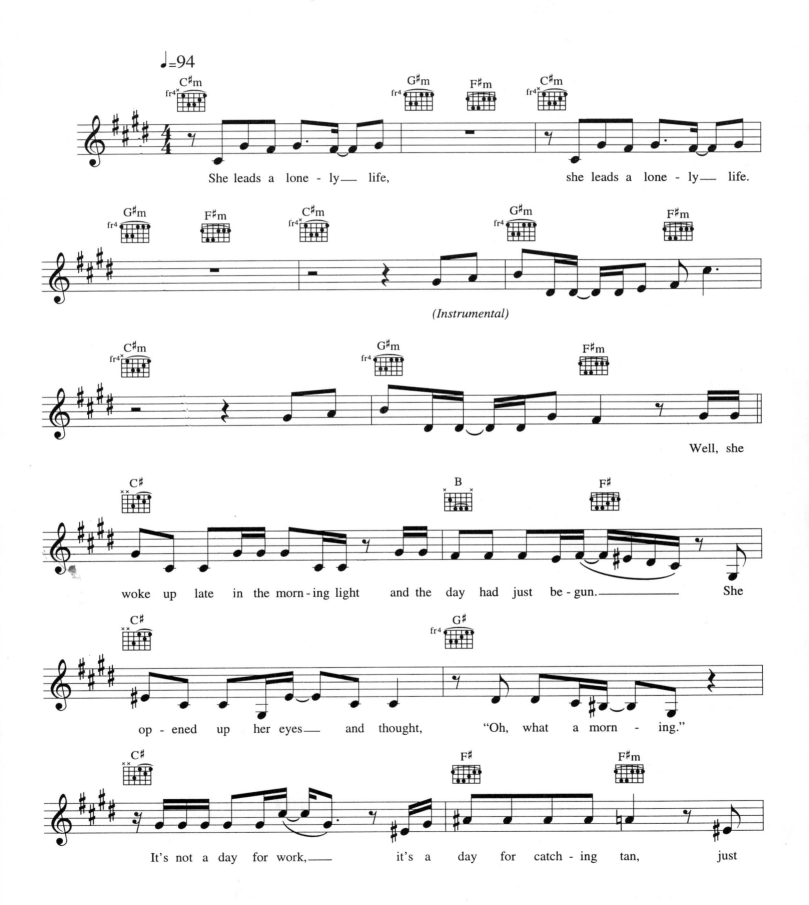

She leads a lone - ly— life, she leads a lone - ly— life.

(Instrumental)

Well, she woke up late in the morn - ing light and the day had just be - gun.___ She op - ened up her eyes— and thought, "Oh, what a morn - ing." It's not a day for work,— it's a day for catch - ing tan, just

ly-ing on the beach— and hav-ing fun.——— She's going to get— ya.

All—— that she wants is—— an-oth-er ba - by. She's gone to-mor - row, boy,

all—— that she wants is—— an-oth-er ba - by, yeah.———

(Instrumental)

All that she wants. So if— you

are in sight and the day is right, she's the hun - ter, you're the fox.———— A

gen - tle voice that talks— to you won't talk for - ev - er.

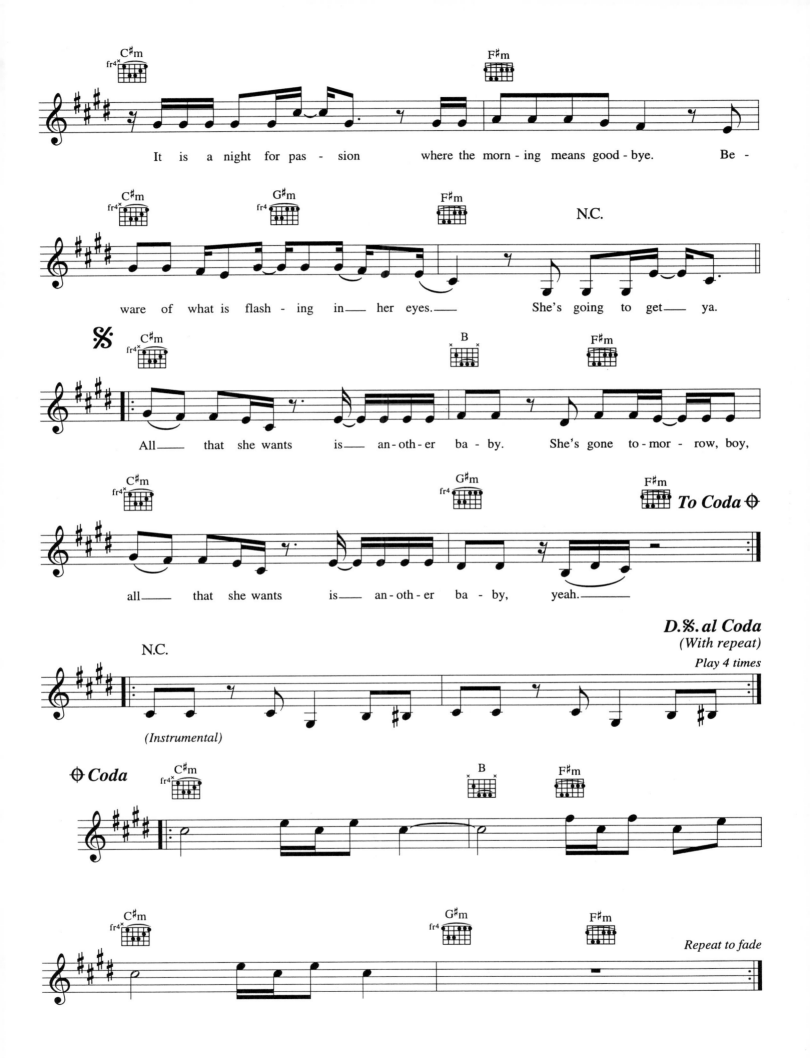

It is a night for pas - sion where the morn - ing means good - bye. Be -

ware of what is flash - ing in her eyes. She's going to get ya.

All that she wants is an - oth - er ba - by. She's gone to - mor - row, boy,

all that she wants is an - oth - er ba - by, yeah.

D.%. al Coda
(With repeat)
Play 4 times

(Instrumental)

Coda

Repeat to fade

5

ALWAYS

Words & Music by Jon Bon Jovi

© Copyright 1994 Jon Bon Jovi Publishing, USA.
PolyGram Music Publishing Limited, 47 British Grove, London W4.
All Rights Reserved. International Copyright Secured.

1. This Ro-me-o is bleed-ing but you can't see his blood,—
   (Verse 2 see block lyric)

it's no-thing but some feel-ings that this old— dog kicked up.—

It's been rain-ing since you left me, now I'm drown-ing in the flood,—

you see I've al-ways been a fight-er, but with-out— you I give up.—

Now I can't sing a love song like the way it's meant to be,— well I

guess I'm not that good a-ny-more,— but ba-by that's— just me.— Yeah,

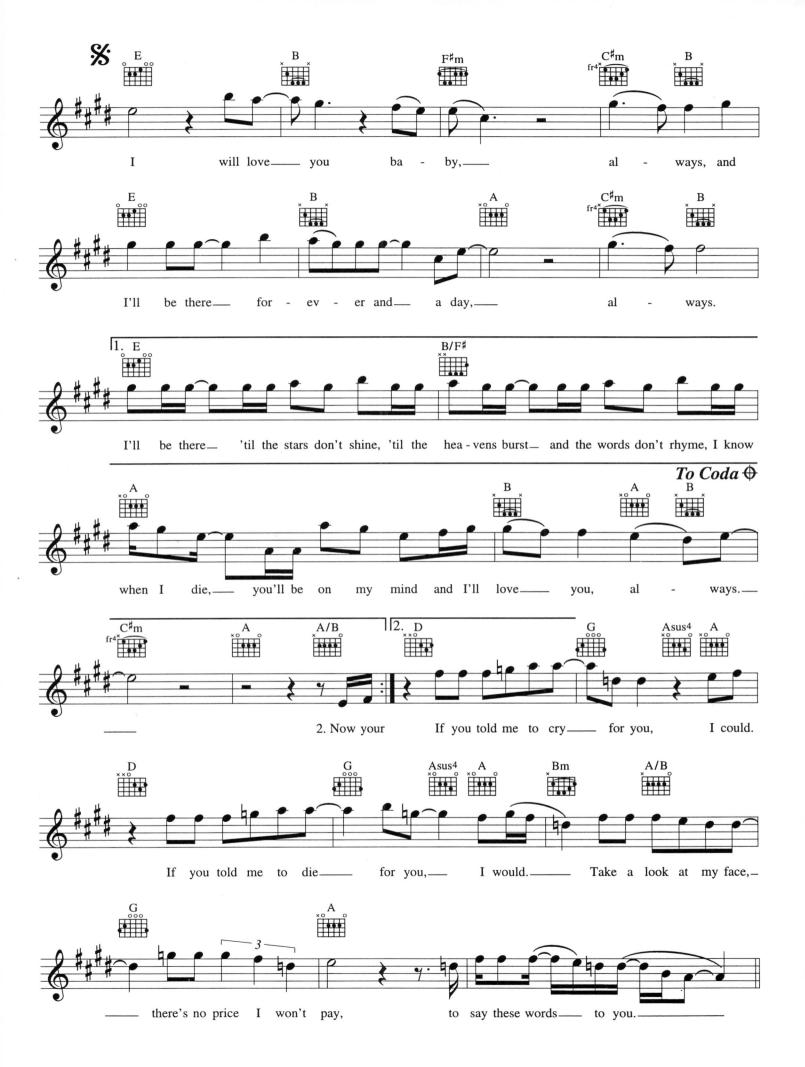

I will love you baby, always, and
I'll be there forever and a day, always.

1. I'll be there 'til the stars don't shine, 'til the heavens burst and the words don't rhyme, I know

To Coda ✛

when I die, you'll be on my mind and I'll love you, always.

2. Now your   If you told me to cry for you, I could.

If you told me to die for you, I would. Take a look at my face,

there's no price I won't pay, to say these words to you.

(Instrumental)

Well there ain't no luck in these load-ed dice,— but ba-by if you give me just one more try,— we can pack up our old dreams and our old lives,— we'll find a place— where the sun still shines, yeah.—

D.%. al Coda

⊕ Coda

Repeat to fade

—— *(Instrumental)*

Verse 2:
Now your pictures that you left behind
Are just memories of a different life,
Some that made us laugh, some that made us cry,
One that made you have to say goodbye.

What I'd give to run my fingers through your hair,
To touch your lips, to hold you near.
When you say your prayers
Try to understand, I've made mistakes, I'm just a man.

When he holds you close, when he pulls you near,
When he says the words you've been needing to hear,
I'll wish I was him, 'cause those words are mine
To say to you 'til the end of time.

BUFFALO SOLDIER

Words & Music by Bob Marley & Noel Williams

© Copyright 1983 Bob Marley Music Limited BV. Controlled for USA and Canada by Almo Music Corporation/Music Sales Corporation, USA.
Rest of the World controlled by Rondor Music Incorporated. Rights for UK and Eire controlled by Windswept Pacific Music Limited, 27 Queensdale Place, London W11 (66.66%)/
Campbell Connelly & Company Limited, 8/9 Frith Street, London W1 (33.33%).
All Rights Reserved. International Copyright Secured.

1. Buf-fa-lo sol-dier, dread-lock Ras-ta. There was a
(Verse 2 see block lyric)

buf-fa-lo sol-dier in the heart of A-mer-i-ca.

Sto-len from Af-ri-ca, brought to A-mer-i-ca.

Fight-ing on ar-ri-val, fight-ing for sur-vi-val, I mean it.

When— I an-a-lyze the stench, to me it makes a lot of sense

how the dread-lock Ras-ta was the buf-fa-lo sol-dier. 2. And he was

who— the heck do I think I am. 3. I'm just a buf-fa-lo sol-dier in the

heart of A-me-ri-ca. Sto-len from Af-ri-ca,

brought to A-me-ri-ca. Said he was fight-ing on ar-ri-val,

fight-ing for sur-vi-val. Said he was the buf-fa-lo sol-dier, win the

war for A-me-ri-ca. Sing-ing: wo-yo-yo, wo-yo-yo-yo;

wo-yo-yo-yo-yo-yo-yo-yo. Buf-fa-lo sol-dier trod-ding through the

land.___ Said you wan-na run and then you make a stand. Trod-ding through the

land,— yeah._____ 4. Said he was a buf - fa - lo sol - dier, win the

(Verse 5 see block lyric)

war for A - mer - i - ca. Buf - fa - lo sol - dier,

dread - lock Ras - ta. Fight - ing on ar - ri - val,

fight - ing for sur - vi - val. Driv - en from the main - land to the

heart of the Car - ib - be - an. Sing - ing: wo - yo - yo, wo - yo - yo - yo;

1. wo - yo - yo - yo - yo - yo - yo - yo. **2.** - yo - yo - yo. ***D.%.*** **3.** - yo - yo - yo. *Repeat to fade*

Verse 2:

And he was taken from Africa, brought to America.
Fighting on arrival, fighting for survival.
Said he was a buffalo soldier dreadlock Rasta
Buffalo soldier in the heart of America.

If you know your history
Then you would know where you're coming from.
Then you wouldn't have to ask me
Who the heck do I think I am.

Verse 5:

Trodding through San Juan in the arms of America.
Trodding through Jamaica, the buffalo soldier.
Fighting on arrival, fighting for survival.
Buffalo soldier, dreadlock Rasta.

CIGARETTES & ALCOHOL

Words & Music by Noel Gallagher

© Copyright 1994 Oasis Music Limited.
Creation Songs Limited/Sony Music Publishing, 10 Great Marlborough Street, London W1.
All Rights Reserved. International Copyright Secured.

1. Is it my——— i - ma - gi - na - tion, or have I fi - nal - ly found——— some-

(Verse 2 see block lyric)

- thing worth liv - ing for?———

I was look - ing for some ac - tion, but all——— I found——— was cig-

- ar - ettes and al - co - hol.———

You could wait for a life - time, to spend your days in the sun -

- shine, you might as well do the white——— line 'cause when it

comes on top,— you got-ta make it hap - pen,— you got-ta make it hap-

- pen,— you got-ta make it hap - pen,— you got-ta make it hap-

- pen.—

2. Is it worth—

(Instrumental)

You got-ta,— you got-ta,— you got-ta make it. You got-ta,— you got-ta,— you got-ta fake it.

Play 4 times

(Instrumental)

Verse 2:
Is it worth the aggravation
To find yourself a job
When there's nothing worth working for?
It's a crazy situation
But all I need
Are cigarettes and alcohol.

COMMON PEOPLE

Music by Pulp
Lyrics by Jarvis Cocker

© Copyright 1994 Island Music Limited, 47 British Grove, London W4.
All Rights Reserved. International Copyright Secured.

♩=152

1. She came from Greece, she had a thirst for know - ledge,
(Verses 2 & 3 see block lyric)

she stud - ied sculp - ture at St. Mar - tin's col - lege, that's where I

caught her eye.

She told me that her

dad was load - ed. I said "In that case, I'll have rum and Co - ca Co - la." She said "Fine."

And then in thir - ty se - conds' time she said

"I want to live like com - mon peo - ple, I want to do what -

ev - er com - mon peo - ple do. Want to sleep with com - mon peo - ple,

I want to sleep with com - mon peo - ple like you." Well, what else

could I do? I said "I'll, I'll see what I can

do." Rent a flat

a - bove a shop, cut your hair and get a job,

smoke some fags and play some pool, pre - tend you ne -

- ver went to school. But still you'll ne - ver get it right

15

'cause when you're laid____ in bed____ at night____ watch-ing roach-

-es climb____ the wall,____ if you called____ your dad____ he could stop____

____ it all,____ yeah. 1. You'll ne-ver live like com-mon peo-ple,
(Chorus 2 see block lyric)

you'll ne-ver do what-ev-er com-mon peo-ple do. You'll ne-ver fail like

com-mon peo-ple, you'll ne-ver watch your life____ slide out of view,____

____ and then dance____ and drink____ and screw____ be-cause there's

To Coda ⊕

noth-ing else____ to do.____

Want to live like com-mon peo - ple like you.

Verse 2:

I took her to the supermarket
I don't know why, but I had to start it somewhere,
So I started there.
I said "Pretend you've got no money."
She just laughed and said "Oh, you're so funny." I said "Yeah?
Well, I can't see anyone else smiling in here.
Are you sure you want to live like common people,
You want to see whatever common people see,
You want to sleep with common people,
You want to sleep with common people like me?"
But she didn't understand, she just smiled and held my hand.

Verse 3:

Like a dog lying in the corner,
They will bite you and never warn you, look out,
They'll tear your insides out.
'Cause everybody hates a tourist,
Especially one who thinks it's all such a laugh
And the chip stains and grease will come out in the bath.
You will never understand how it feels
To live your life with no meaning or control
And with nowhere left to go.
You're amazed that they exist
And they burn so bright while you can only wonder why.

Chorus 2:

Sing along with the common people,
Sing along and it might just get you through.
Laugh along with the common people,
Laugh along, even though they're laughing at you
And the stupid things that you do
Becuase you think that poor is cool.

COUNTRY HOUSE

Words & Music by Damon Albarn, Graham Coxon, Alex James & David Rowntree

© Copyright 1995 MCA Music Limited, 77 Fulham Palace Road, London W6.
All Rights Reserved. International Copyright Secured.

lives   in   a   house,   a   ve - ry   big   house   in   the   coun   -   try,

watch - ing   af - ter - noon   re - peats   and   the   food   he   eats___   in   the   coun -

- try.   He   takes   all   man - ner   of   pills___   and   piles   up

a - na - lyst's   bills___   in   the   coun   -   try;   ooh, ___   it's   like   an

An - i - mal   Farm, ___   lots   of   ru - ral   charm___   in   the   coun   -   try.

2. He's   got   In   the   coun   -   try,

D.C. al Coda

in   the   coun   -   try,   in   the   coun - try. ___

⊕ *Coda*

(Instrumental)

Blow,   blow   me   out,____

____ I am____ so sad,____ I don't____

____ know why.____   Oh,____ he

CHORUS

lives in a house, a ve - ry big house in the

(Chorus 2 see block lyric)

coun - try,   watch - ing af - ter - noon re - peats and the

food he eats____ in the coun - try.   He takes all

man - ner of pills____ and piles up a - na - lyst's bills____ in the coun - try;

ooh, _____ it's like an An - i - mal Farm, _____ lots of ru - ral charm _____ in the coun-

1. A
- try. Oh, _____ he -

2. A
ry. _____ Ooh, la la

A
la. *(Instrumental)*

D7   A   E Eb E

Repeat to fade

Verse 2:

He's got morning glory,
And life's a different story;
Everything's going 'Jackanory'...
In touch with his own mortality.
He's reading Balzac, knocking back Prozac—
It's a helping hand that makes you feel wonderfully bland;
Oh, it's the century's remedy:
For the faint at heart, a new start.

Chorus 2:

He lives in a house, a very big house in the country,
He's got a fog in his chest
So it needs a lot of rest in the country.
He doesn't drink, smoke, laugh;
Takes herbal baths in the country.
But you'll come to no harm
On the Animal Farm in the country.

Verse 3: Instrumental

DISCO 2000

Music by Pulp
Lyrics by Jarvis Cocker

© Copyright 1995 Island Music Limited, 47 British Grove, London W4.
All Rights Reserved. International Copyright Secured.

♩=138

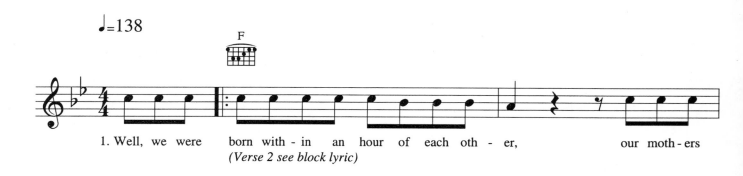

1. Well, we were born with-in an hour of each oth-er, our moth-ers
(Verse 2 see block lyric)

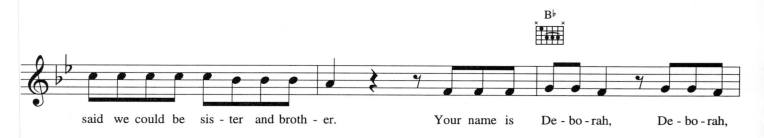

said we could be sis-ter and broth-er. Your name is De-bo-rah, De-bo-rah,

it ne-ver suit-ed ya. And they

said that when we grew up we'd get mar-ried and ne-ver split up.
(D.𝄋 instrumental)

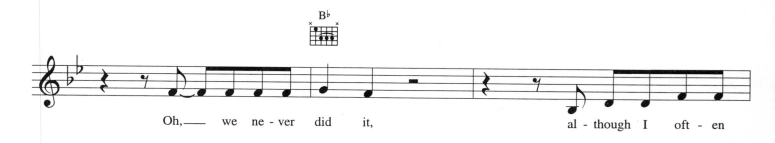

Oh,— we ne-ver did it, al-though I oft-en

(Vocal each time)

thought of it. Oh, Deb - 'rah, do you re - call?

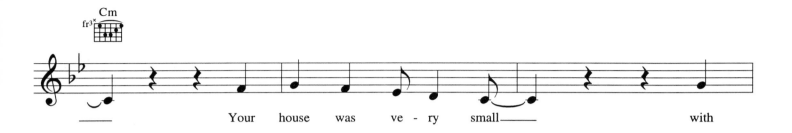

Cm

Your house was ve - ry small with

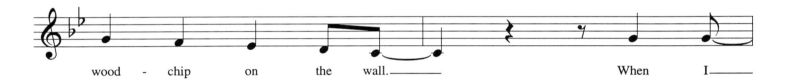

wood - chip on the wall. When I

came round to call you did - n't no -

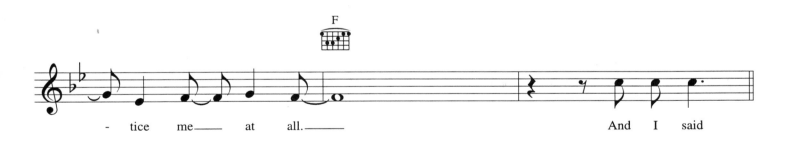

F

- tice me at all. And I said

B♭

"Let's all meet up in the year two thou - sand,

23

$\oplus$ *Coda*

What are you do - in' Sun - day, ba - by?

Would you like to come and meet——— me, may - be? You can ev - en bring———

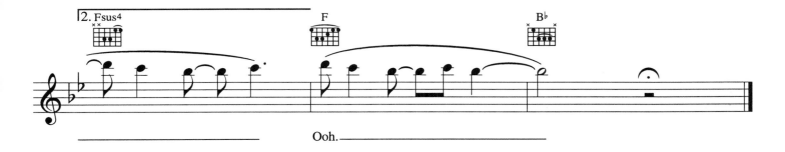

——— your ba - by.   Ooh.———

1.

——————— Ooh.———

2.

Verse 2:

You were the first girl at school to get breasts,
Martyn said that yours were the best.
The boys all loved you but then I was a mess,
I had to watch them trying to get you undressed.
We were friends but that was as far as it went,
I used to walk you home sometimes but
It meant nothing to you
'Cause you were so popular.

DOWN ON THE FARM

Words & Music by Charles Harper, Alvin Gibbs & Nicholas Garrett

© Copyright 1980 The Sparta Florida Music Group Limited, 8/9 Frith Street, London W1.
All Rights Reserved. International Copyright Secured.

(Rhythm guitar plays melody)

1. *(Spoken)* All I need is some inspiration before I do somebody some harm. I
(Verse 2 see block lyric)

feel just like a vegetable down here on the farm. 2. No-

(Instrumental)

3. Nobody comes to see me, nobody here to turn me on. I
(Verses 4, 5 & 6 see block lyric)

To Coda ⊕

ain't even got a lover down here on the farm.

D.%. al Coda
Play 4 times

(Guitar solo ad lib.)

⊕ *Coda*

7. I can't fall in love with a wheatfield,   I can't   fall   in   love   with   a   barn.   Well,
(Verse 8 see block lyric)

everything smells like horseshit   down here on the farm.

(Instrumental)

Verse 2:
Nobody comes to see me,
Nobody here to turn me on.
I ain't even got a lover
Down here on the farm.

Verse 4:
Drinkin' lemonade shandy,
Ain't nobody here to do me harm.
But I'm like a fish out of water
Down here on the farm.

Verse 5 (%):
I wrote a thousand letters
'Til my fingers all gone numb,
But I never see no postman
Down here on the farm.

Verse 6:
I call my baby on the telephone, I say
Come down and have some fun,
But she knows what the score is
Down here on the farm.

Verse 8 (⊕ Coda):

Blue skies and swimming pools
Add so much charm,
But I'd rather be back in Soho
Than down here on the farm.

DREAMS

Words by Dolores O'Riordan
Music by Dolores O'Riordan & Noel Hogan

© Copyright 1992 Island Music Limited, 47 British Grove, London W4.
All Rights Reserved. International Copyright Secured.

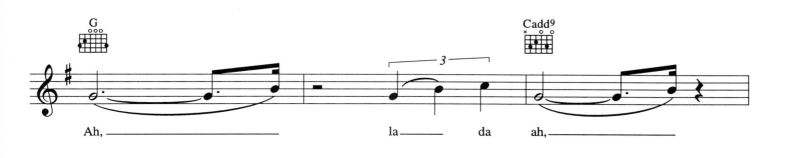

Ah, _____ la ___ da ah, _____

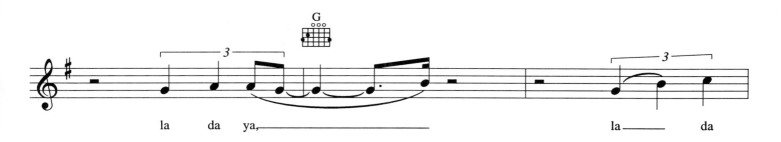

la da ya, _____ la ___ da

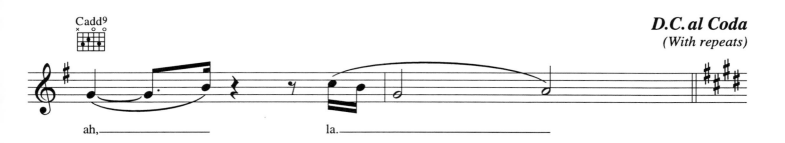

D.C. al Coda
(With repeats)

ah, _____ la. _____

⊕ Coda

Oh, my life is
And oh, my dreams, it's

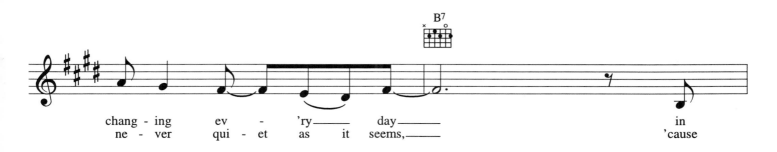

chang - ing ev - 'ry ___ day ___ in
ne - ver qui - et as it seems, ___ 'cause

1.

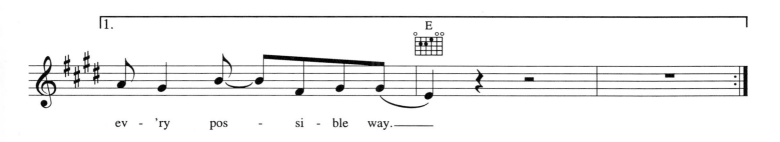

ev - 'ry pos - si - ble way. ___

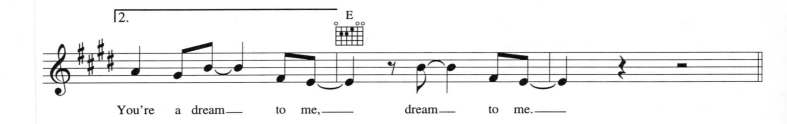

You're a dream— to me,— dream— to me.—

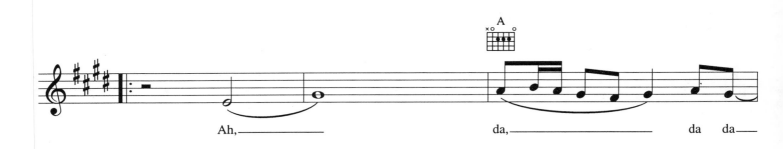

Ah,——— da,——— da da—

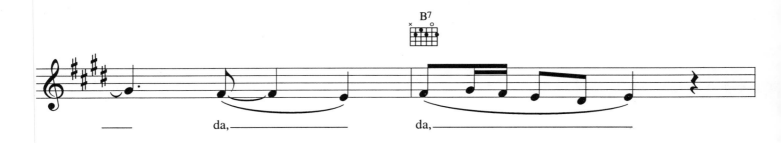

— da,——— da,———

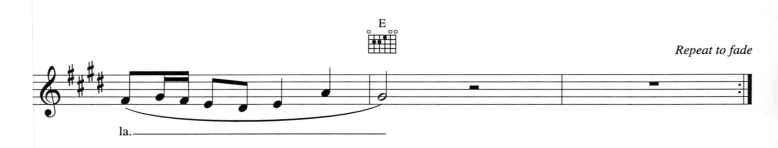

Repeat to fade

la.———

Verse 3:
I want more, impossible to ignore,
Impossible to ignore.
And they'll come true, impossible not to do,
Impossible not to do.

Verse 4:
And now I tell you openly, you have my heart so don't hurt me.
You're what I couldn't find.
A totally amazing mind, so understanding and so kind;
You're everything to me.

EVERYTHING I SAID

Words by Dolores O'Riordan
Music by Dolores O'Riordan & Noel Hogan

© Copyright 1994 Island Music Limited, 47 British Grove, London W4.
All Rights Reserved. International Copyright Secured.

Gently

1. It makes me lone - ly, _____ it makes me ve - ry lone -
(Verse 2 see block lyric)

- ly when I see _____ you here, _____ wait - in' on. _____

1. But you have _____

CHORUS

_____ your _____ heart, _____ oh, _____ don't be - lieve _____ it, _____
(Chorus 2 see block lyric)

and you ran _____ out - side, _____ wait - ing on. _____

da;＿＿＿＿＿＿＿＿＿ la,＿＿ da, da,＿＿ da, da, da, da;

la,＿＿ da, da,＿＿ da, da, da;＿＿＿＿＿＿＿

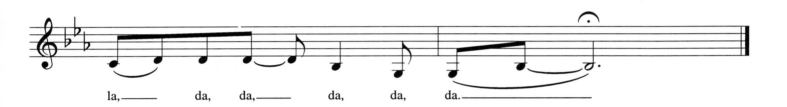

la,＿＿ da, da,＿＿ da, da, da.＿＿＿＿＿＿

Verse 2:

It makes me tired, it makes me very tired
And inside of me, lingers on.

Chorus 2:

Everything I said, oh, well I meant it,
And inside my head, holdin' on.

Bridge 2:

And if I lied in spite, would you still be here,
No, would you disappear?

Verse 4:

I'll get over you, I'll get over you,
But I don't make you lonely.

FIELDS OF GOLD

Words & Music by Sting

© Copyright 1993 G. M. Sumner. Magnetic Publishing Limited, London W1.
All Rights Reserved. International Copyright Secured.

the fields___ of gold.   2. Will you

I nev-er made prom-is-es light-ly   and there have been

some that I've bro-ken,   but I swear___ in the days still left we'll walk___

___ in fields___ of gold.   We'll___ walk in fields___ of gold.

(Instrumental)

Verse 3:
Will you stay with me, will you be my love
Among the fields of barley?
We'll forget the sun in his jealous sky
As we walk in fields of gold.

Verse 4:
See the west wind move like a lover so
Upon the fields of barley.
Feel her body rise as you kiss her mouth
Among the fields of gold.

Verse 6:
You'll remember me when the west wind moves
Upon the fields of barley.
You can tell the sun in his jealous sky
When we walked in fields of gold.

GIRLS AND BOYS

Words & Music by Damon Albarn, Graham Coxon, Alex James & David Rowntree

© Copyright 1994 MCA Music Limited, 77 Fulham Palace Road, London W6.
All Rights Reserved. International Copyright Secured.

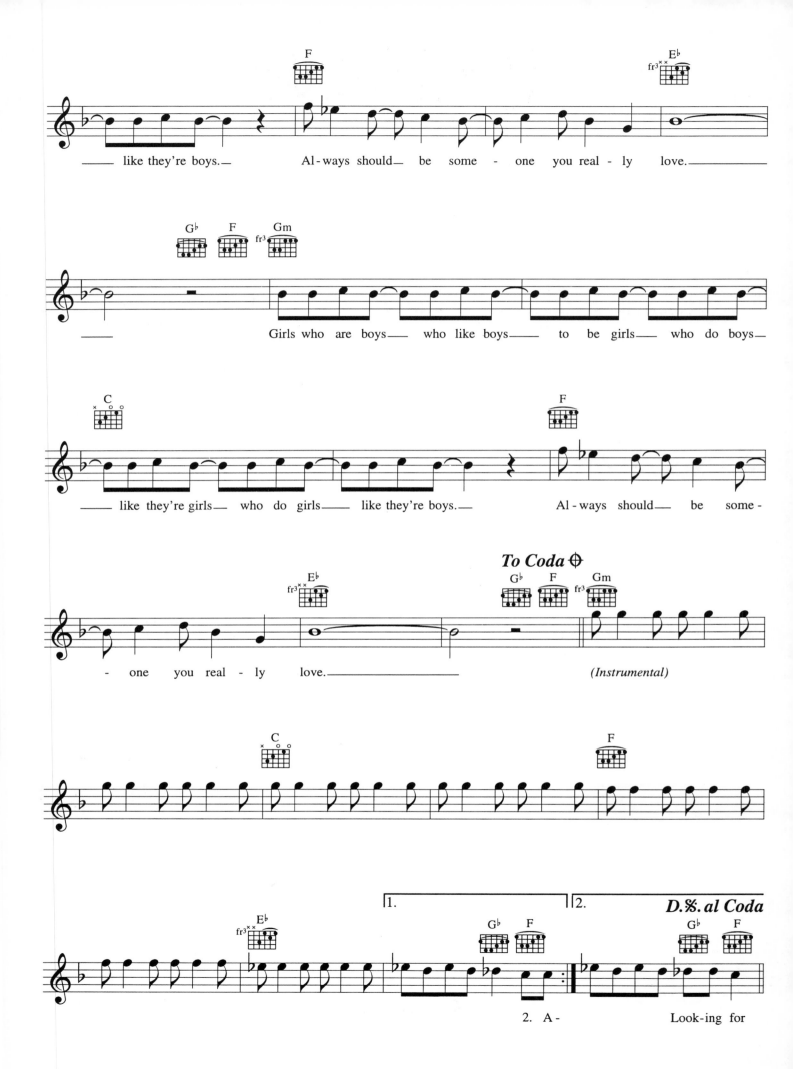

like they're boys. Al-ways should be some - one you real - ly love.

Girls who are boys who like boys to be girls who do boys

like they're girls who do girls like they're boys. Al - ways should be some -

To Coda ⊕

- one you real - ly love. *(Instrumental)*

1.

2.

D.%. al Coda

2. A - Look-ing for

⊕ *Coda*

Girls who are boys —— who like boys —— to be girls —— who do boys ——

—— like they're girls —— who do girls —— like they're boys. —— Al - ways should —— be some -

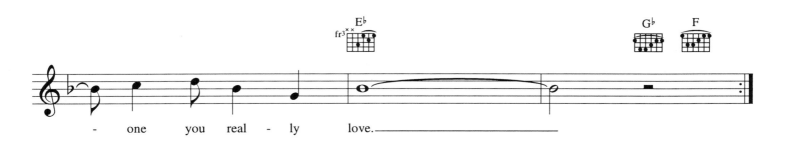

- one you real - ly love. ————————————

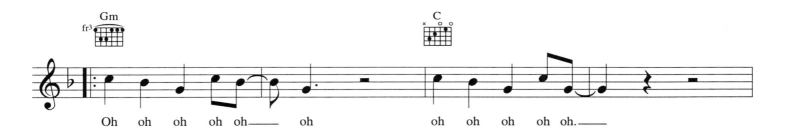

Oh oh oh oh oh —— oh oh oh oh oh oh. ——

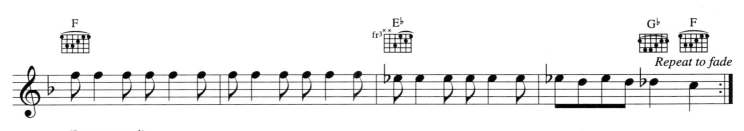

Repeat to fade

(Instrumental)

Verse 2:

Avoiding all work
Because there's none available.
Like battery thinkers
Count their thoughts on 1 2 3 4 5 fingers.
Nothing is wasted,
Only reproduced,
You get nasty blisters
Du bist sehr schön,
But we haven't been introduced.

GOLDENEYE
(THEME FROM THE JAMES BOND FILM)

Words & Music by Bono & The Edge

© Copyright 1995 Blue Mountain Music Limited, 47 British Grove, London W4.
All Rights Reserved. International Copyright Secured.

♩=104

1. See re - flec - tions on the wa - ter, more than dark - ness
(Verse 2 see block lyric)

in the depths.— See him sur - face and ne - ver a sha - dow,

on the wind I feel his breath. Gold - en - eye, I've

found his weak - ness. Gold - en - eye, he'll do what I please.—

Gold - en - eye, no time for sweet - ness, but a bit - ter kiss— will bring him

to his knees.— You'll ne - ver know— how I've

Re - venge!_____ It's a kiss, this time I won't miss

now I've got you in my sight._____

With a gold - en eye,_____ Gold - en

Gold - en - eye._____ With a gold - en eye,_____

Gold - en - eye._____ *(Instrumental)*

Verse 2:
See him move through smoke and mirrors,
Feel his presence in the crowd.
Other girls, they gather round him,
If I had him I wouldn't let him out.
Goldeneye, my lace for leather,
Golden chain break him to the spot.
Goldeneye, I'll show him forever,
It'll take forever to see what I've got.

You'll never know how I watched you from the shadows as a child.
You'll never know how it feels to get so close and be denied.

Has My Fire Really Gone Out?

Words & Music by Paul Weller

© Copyright 1993 Notting Hill Music (UK) Limited.
All Rights Reserved. International Copyright Secured.

has my fi - re real - ly, real - ly gone out?

(Instrumental)

Some - thing real is what I'm seek - ing,
(Vocal 1º only)

one clear voice in the wil - der - ness.

(Instrumental)

Play 3 times

(Repeat ad lib.)

HAPPY NATION

Words & Music by Buddha & Joker

© Copyright 1992 Megasong Publishing, Sweden.
PolyGram Music Publishing Limited, 47 British Grove, London W4.
All Rights Reserved. International Copyright Secured.

♩=88

Hap-py na-tion, liv-in' in a hap-py na-tion,____

where the peo-ple un-der-stand and dream of per-fect,

mad si-tu-a-tion. Lead to sweet sal-va-tion____

for the peo-ple, for the good, for man-kind, broth-er-

hood.

I-deas by____ man, and on-ly what will last.____

hood.

(Instrumental)

Tell them we've gone— too far.—

Tell them we've gone— too far.—

(Hap - py na - tion) Come through and I will dance with you.—

(Hap - py na - tion ———) Tell them we've gone— too far.—

(Hap - py na - tion) Come through and I will dance with you.———

——— (Hap - py na - tion———) Tell them we've gone— too far.—

D.%. al Coda

Come through and I will dance with you.———

⊕ Coda

Hap - - py na - tion.———

Hap - - py na - - tion.———

HAVE I TOLD YOU LATELY

Words & Music by Van Morrison

© Copyright 1989 Essential Music. PolyGram Music Publishing Limited, 47 British Grove, London W4.
All Rights Reserved. International Copyright Secured.

Verse 2:

Oh the morning sun in all its glory
Greets the day with hope and comfort too.
And you fill my life with laughter,
You can make it better.

Verse 3: — as Verse 1

Verse 4: — Instrumental

Verse 5: — as Verse 1

ISRAELITES

Words & Music by Desmond Dacres & Leslie Kong

© Copyright 1969 The Sparta Florida Music Group Limited, 8/9 Frith Street, London W1 (25%)/
Blue Mountain Music Limited, 47 British Grove, London W4 (75%).
All Rights Reserved. International Copyright Secured.

♩=102

1, 3. Get up in the morn-ing, slav-ing for bread, sir,
(Verse 2 see block lyric)

so that-a ev-er-y mouth can be fed.

Oh,

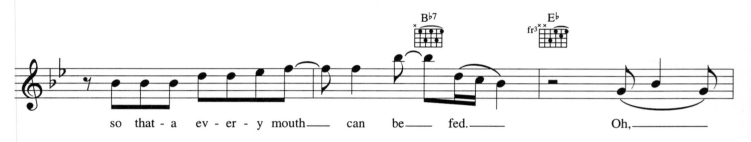

oh, the Is-rael-ites.

My

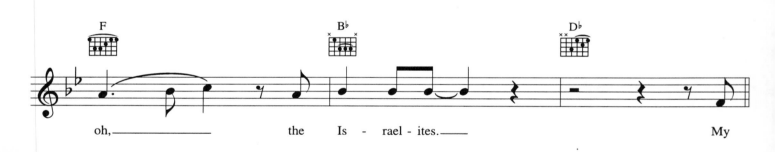

wife and my kids they pack up and a-leave me.

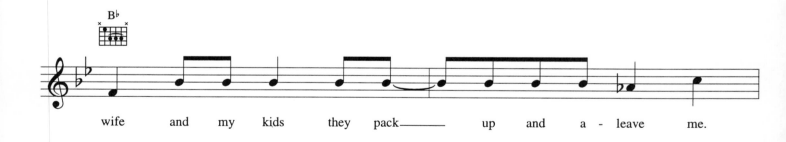

"Dar-ling" she said "I was yours to re-ceive".

Oh,

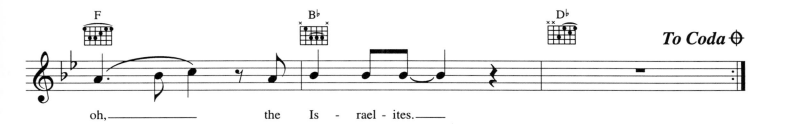

oh,_____ the Is - rael - ites._____

(Instrumental)

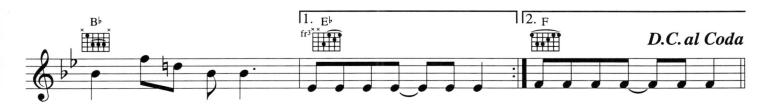

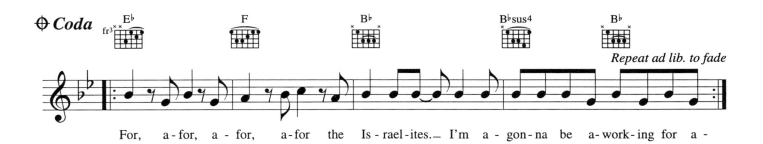

For, a-for, a-for, a-for the Is-rael-ites.— I'm a-gon-na be a-work-ing for a-

Verse 2:
Shirt dem a tear up, trousers are gone,
I don't want to end up like Bonnie and Clyde.
Oh, oh, the Israelites.
After a storm there must be a calming,
Catch me in a farm they stone you alive.
Working for, a-for, a-for the Israelites.

KEEP THE FAITH

Words & Music by Jon Bon Jovi, Richie Sambora & Desmond Child

© Copyright 1992 PolyGram International Music Incorporated/Bon Jovi Publishing/Aggressive Music/EMI April Music Incorporated/Desmobile Music Company, USA.
EMI Songs Limited, 127 Charing Cross Road, London WC2 (33.33%)/PolyGram Music Publishing Limited, 47 British Grove, London W4 (66.66%).
All Rights Reserved. International Copyright Secured.

1. Mo - ther, mo - ther, tell your chil - dren that their time has just_ be - gun._ I have suf - fered for my an - ger,_ there are wars_ that can't_ be won._ Fa - ther, fa - ther, please be - lieve_ me, I am lay - ing down_ my guns._ I am

(Verse 2 see block lyric)

bro - ken_ like an ar - row,_ for - give me,_ for - give your way - ward son._

Ev - 'ry - bo - dy needs some - bo - dy to love,_ ev - 'ry - bo - dy needs some -

(D.§. see block lyric)

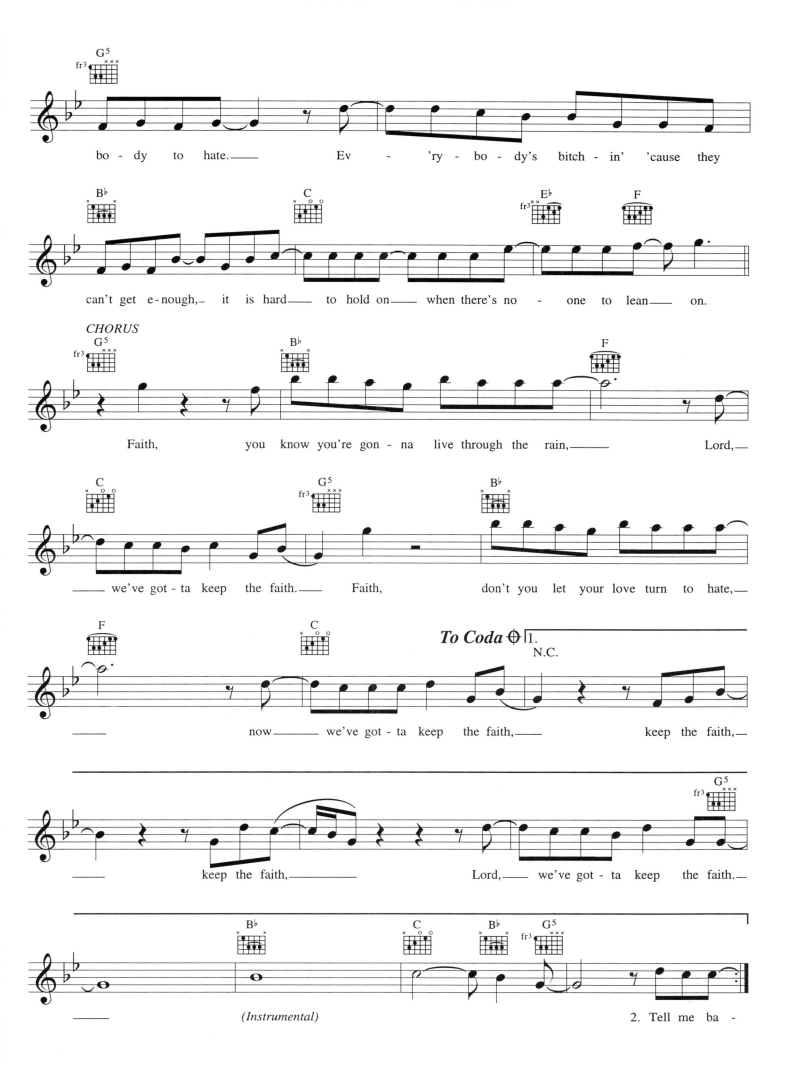

faith, don't you let your love turn to hate,——— Lord,———

——— you've got-ta keep the faith,——— keep the faith,——— keep the faith,—

———————— oh——— we've got-ta keep the faith,——— keep the faith,—

——— keep the faith,——————— Lord,——— we've got-ta keep the faith.—

——— *(Instrumental)* Yeah, yeah, yeah.

Play 3 times

(Guitar solo)

(Spoken) I've been

walk-in' in the foot-steps of so-ci-e-ty's lies, — I don't

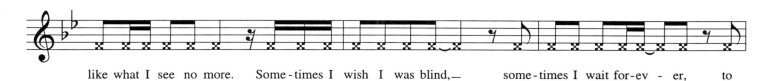

like what I see no more. Some-times I wish I was blind,— some-times I wait for-ev-er, to

D.%. al Coda

stand out in the rain, — so no-one sees me cry-in' tryin' to wash a-way— this pain. Mo-ther, fa-

⊕ Coda

_____ keep the faith, _____ keep the faith—

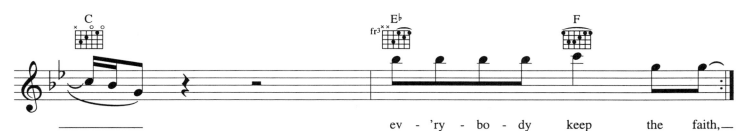

_____ ev-'ry-bo-dy keep the faith,—

Verse 2:
Tell me baby, when I hurt you
Do you keep it all inside?
Do you tell me all's forgiven
Or just hide behind your pride?

Everybody needs somebody to love,
Everybody needs somebody to hate.
Everybody's bitchin' 'cause the time are tough,
Well it's hard to be strong when there's no one to dream on.

Chorus 2:
Faith, you know you're gonna live through the rain,
Lord, we've gotta keep the faith.
Faith, don't you know it's never too late,
Right now we've gotta keep the faith.

D.%.

Mother, father, there are things I can't erase.
Every night we fall from grace.
Hard with the world in your face,
Try to hold on, try to hold on.

LIVIN' ON A PRAYER

Words & Music by Jon Bon Jovi, Richie Sambora & Desmond Child

© Copyright 1986 Bon Jovi Publishing/EMI April Music Incorporated/Desmobile Music Company Incorporated/PolyGram Music Publishing Incorporated, USA.
PolyGram Music Publishing Limited, 47 British Grove, London W4 (66.66%)/EMI Songs Limited, 127 Charing Cross Road, London WC2 (33.33%).
All Rights Reserved. International Copyright Secured.

1. Tom-my used to work on the docks,_____ Un-ion's been on strike, he's
(Verse 2 see block lyric)

down on his luck, it's tough,_____ so tough._____

Gi-na works the di-ner all day,_____ work-ing for her man, she

brings home_ her pay for love,_____ for love._____

She says we've got to hold_ on_ to what we've got 'cause it

does-n't make a diff-'rence if we make it or not. We've got each oth-er and

Em · · · that's a lot for — love, we'll give it a shot.

Oh, we're half way — there, — oh — liv -

- in' on a prayer. — Take my — hand, — we'll make it I swear, —

oh, — liv - in' on a prayer. —

Liv - in' on — a prayer. — We've got to hold — on, —

read - y or — not, you live for the fight when it's all that you've got.

Verse 2:

Tommy got his six-string in hock,
Now he's holding in when he used to make it talk so tough,
It's tough.
Gina dreams of running away,
When she cries in the night Tommy whispers, baby it's O.K.
Some day.

LINGER

Words by Dolores O'Riordan
Music by Dolores O'Riordan & Noel Hogan

© Copyright 1992 Island Music Limited, 47 British Grove, London W4.
All Rights Reserved. International Copyright Secured.

Moderately (not too fast)

Verse 2:
If you, if you could get by trying not to lie,
Things wouldn't be so confused
And I wouldn't feel so used,
But you always really knew
I just wanna be with you.

LOVE IS ALL AROUND

Words & Music by Reg Presley

© Copyright 1967 Dick James Music Limited, 47 British Grove, London W4.
All Rights Reserved. International Copyright Secured.

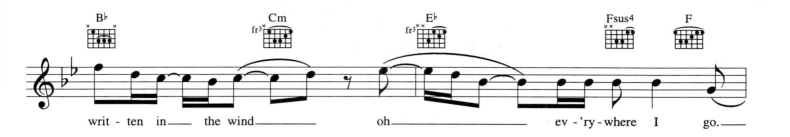

writ - ten in___ the wind_____ oh_____ ev -'ry-where I go.___

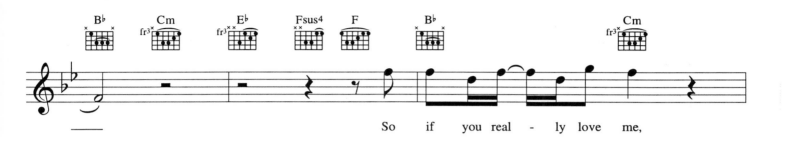

___ So if you real - ly love me,

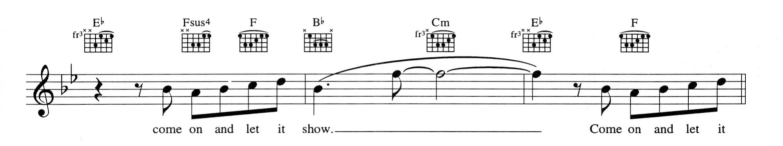

come on and let it show._____ Come on and let it

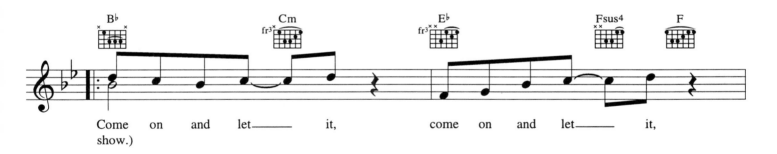

Come on and let___ it, come on and let___ it,
show.)

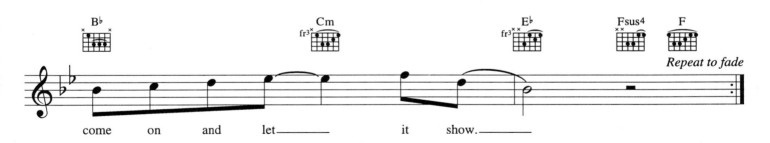

Repeat to fade

come on and let_____ it show._____

Verse 2:

I see your face before me
As I lay on my bed;
I cannot get to thinking
Of all the things you said.
You gave your promise to me
And I gave mine to you;
I need someone beside me
In everything I do.

MIS-SHAPES

Music by Pulp
Lyrics by Jarvis Cocker

© Copyright 1995 Island Music Limited, 47 British Grove, London W4.
All Rights Reserved. International Copyright Secured.

Mis - shapes, mis - takes, mis - fits, raised on a di - et of

bro - ken bis - cuits, oh. We don't look the same as you——

and we don't do the things you do,—— but we live round— here too.——

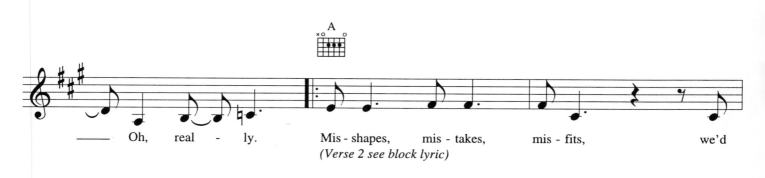

—— Oh, real - ly. Mis - shapes, mis - takes, mis - fits, we'd
(Verse 2 see block lyric)

like to go to town but we—— can't risk—— it, oh, 'cause they just want to

keep us out,___ you could end up with a smash in the mouth___

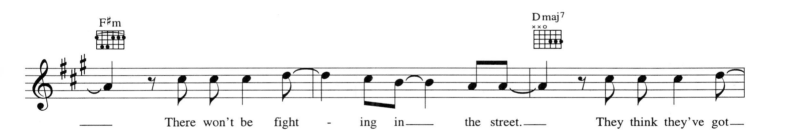

just for stand - ing out,___ now, real - ly. Broth - er, sis -

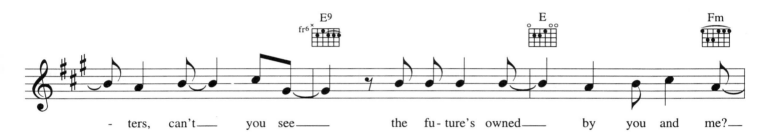

- ters, can't___ you see___ the fu - ture's owned___ by you and me?___

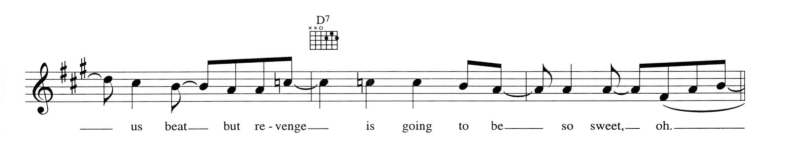

___ There won't be fight - ing in___ the street.___ They think they've got___

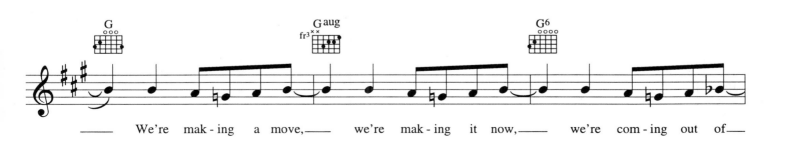

___ us beat___ but re - venge___ is going to be___ so sweet,___ oh.___

___ We're mak - ing a move,___ we're mak - ing it now,___ we're com - ing out of___

_____ the side - lines.   Just   put   your   hands_____ up,   it's   a   raid.

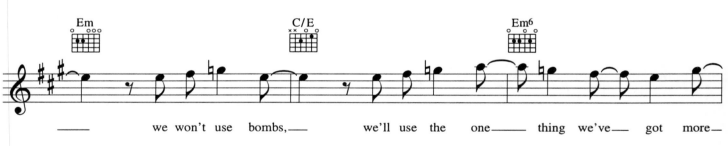

_____   We   want   your   homes,_____   we   want   your   lives,_____

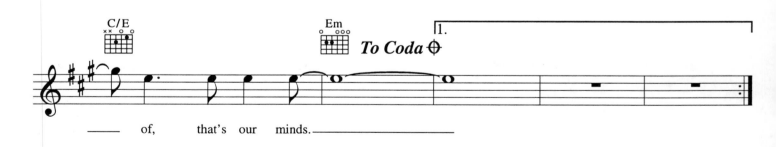

_____   we   want   the   things_____   you   won't   al - low_____   us.   We   won't   use   guns,

_____   we   won't   use   bombs,_____   we'll   use   the   one_____   thing   we've_____   got   more_____

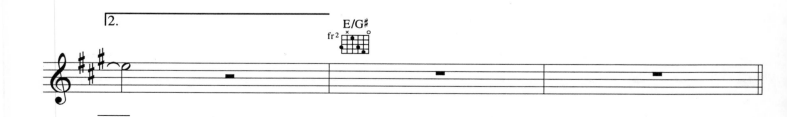

_____   of,   that's   our   minds._____

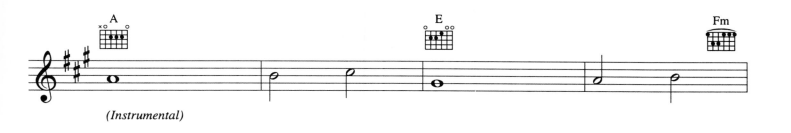

(Instrumental)

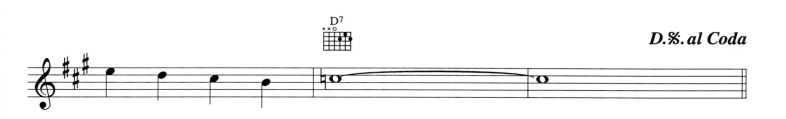

D.%. al Coda

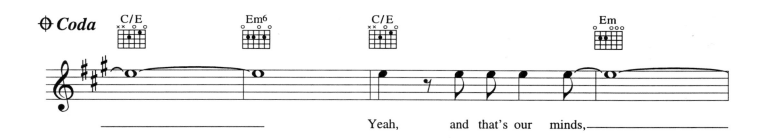

Yeah,   and that's our minds,

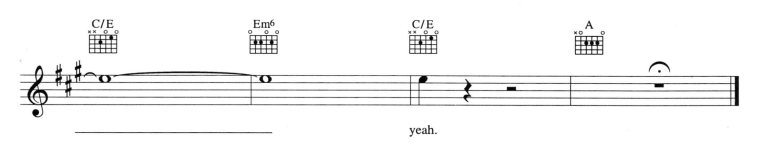

yeah.

Verse 2:
Check your lucky numbers,
That much money could drag you under, oh.
What's the point of being rich
If you can't think of what to do with it
'Cause you're so bleedin thick?
Oh, we weren't supposed to be,
We learned too much at school.
Now we can't help but see
The future that you've got mapped out
Is nothing much to shout about.

MISSING

Music by Ben Watt
Words by Tracey Thorn

© Copyright 1994 Sony Music Publishing, 10 Great Marlborough Street, London W1.
All Rights Reserved. International Copyright Secured.

des - erts miss the rain.

Coda

and I miss

you. you've found some bet - ter place. And I miss you

like the des - erts miss the rain, and I miss you

Repeat to fade

like the des - erts miss the rain. And I miss you

Verse 2:

Could you be dead?
You always were two steps ahead of everyone.
We'd walk behind while you would run.
I look up at your house
And I can almost hear you shout down to me
Where I always used to be.
And I miss you.

Verse 3:

Back on the train
I ask why did I come again?
Can I confess I've been hanging 'round your old address
And the years have proved
To offer nothing since you moved.
You're long gone but I can't move on.
And I miss you.

Verse 4:

I step off the train,
I'm walking down your street again
And past your door, but you don't live there anymore.
It's years since you've been there,
And now you've disappeared somewhere,
Like outer space, you've found some better place.
And I miss you.

71

MORNING GLORY

Words & Music by Noel Gallagher

© Copyright 1995 Oasis Music Limited.
Creation Songs/Sony Music Publishing, 10 Great Marlborough Street, London W1.
All Rights Reserved. International Copyright Secured.

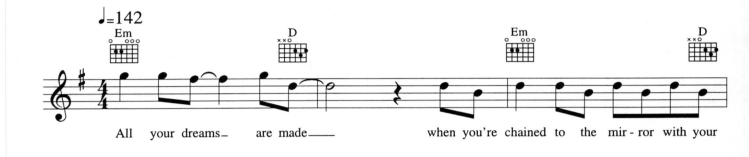

All your dreams— are made—— when you're chained to the mir-ror with your

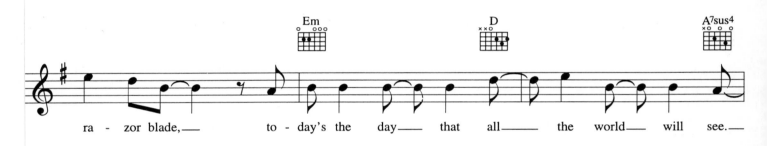

ra - zor blade,— to - day's the day— that all— the world— will see.

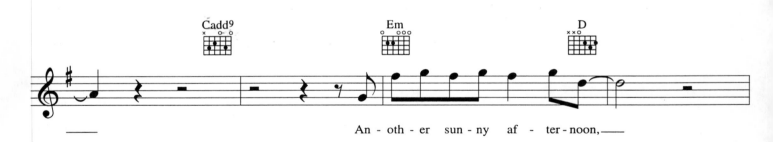

—— An - oth - er sun - ny af - ter - noon,—

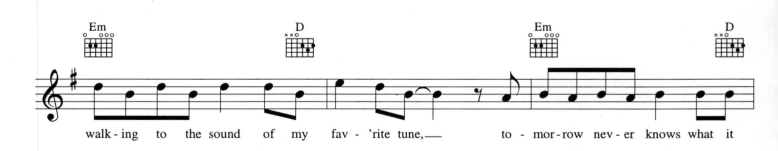

walk - ing to the sound of my fav - 'rite tune,— to - mor - row nev - er knows what it

does - n't know— too soon.—

Need a lit-tle time to wake___ up, need a lit-tle time to wake___

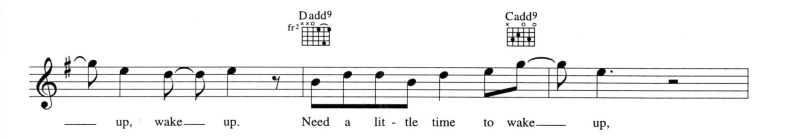

___ up, wake___ up. Need a lit-tle time to wake___ up,

need a lit-tle time to rest___ your mind,___ you know you should,___ so I guess___

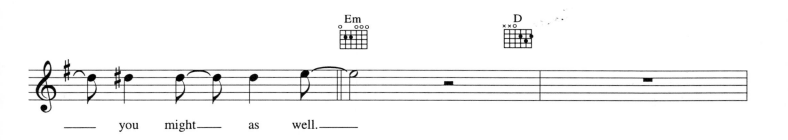

___ you might___ as well.___

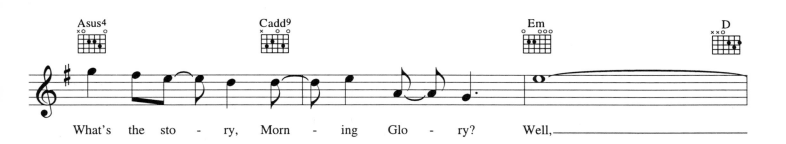

What's the sto - ry, Morn - ing Glo - ry? Well,___

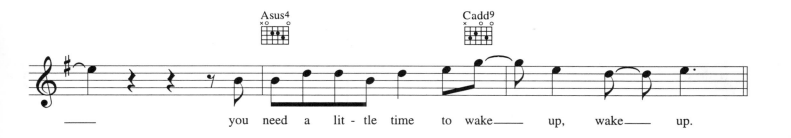

___ you need a lit-tle time to wake___ up, wake___ up.

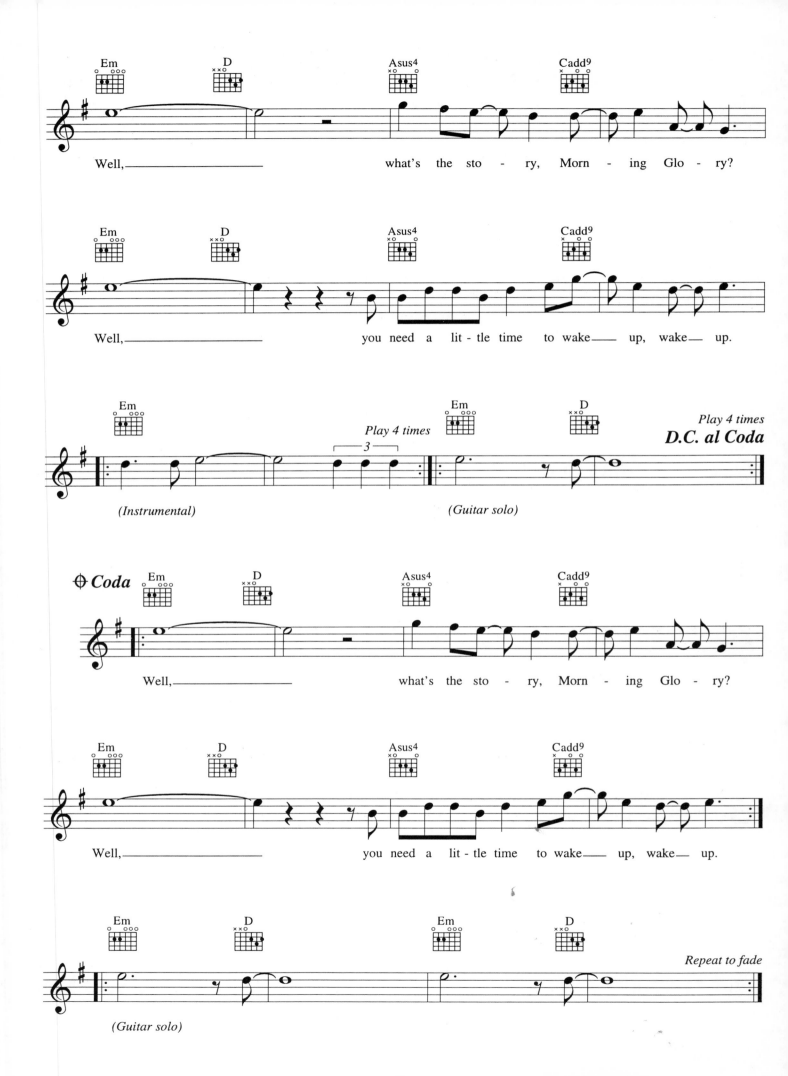

Well,_____ what's the sto - ry, Morn - ing Glo - ry?

Well,_____ you need a lit - tle time to wake___ up, wake___ up.

(Instrumental)

Play 4 times

┌─ 3 ─┐

Play 4 times
D.C. al Coda

(Guitar solo)

⊕ *Coda*

Well,_____ what's the sto - ry, Morn - ing Glo - ry?

Well,_____ you need a lit - tle time to wake___ up, wake___ up.

Repeat to fade

(Guitar solo)

NEED YOU TONIGHT

Words & Music by Andrew Farriss & Michael Hutchence

© Copyright 1987 MMA Music International for Australasia.
Published by PolyGram International Music Publishing B.V. for the Rest of the World. PolyGram Music Publishing Limited,
47 British Grove, London W4. Published by ToyBox Publishing for Japan.
All Rights Reserved. International Copyright Secured.

Verses 2 & 3:
I need you tonight
'Cause I'm not sleeping,
There's something 'bout you girl
That makes me sweat.

NO NEED TO ARGUE

Words & Music by Dolores O'Riordan

© Copyright 1994 Island Music Limited, 47 British Grove, London W4.
All Rights Reserved. International Copyright Secured.

Verse 2:

And I remember all the things we once shared,
Watching T. V. movies on the living room armchair.
But they say it will work out fine.
Was it all a waste of time
'Cause I knew, I knew I'd lose you?
You'll always be special to me,
Special to me, to me.

NEVER TEAR US APART

Words & Music by Andrew Farriss & Michael Hutchence

© Copyright 1987 MMA Music International for Australasia.
Published by PolyGram International Music Publishing B.V. for the Rest of the World. PolyGram Music Publishing Limited,
47 British Grove, London W4. Published by ToyBox Publishing for Japan.
All Rights Reserved. International Copyright Secured.

Don't ask me —— what you know is true, —— don't have to tell you —— I love your—— pre-cious heart.—— I, I was stand-ing, you were there, two worlds col-li-ded—— and they could nev-er tear us a-part.

We could

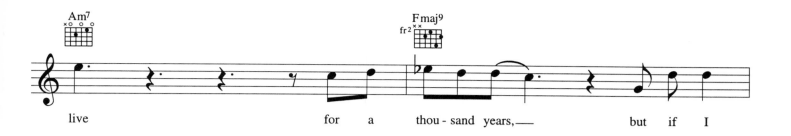

live   for a thou - sand years, but if I

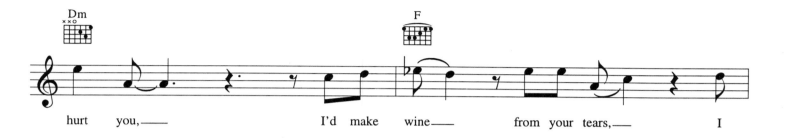

hurt you,   I'd make wine from your tears, I

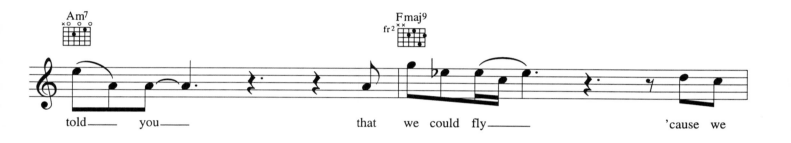

told you   that we could fly 'cause we

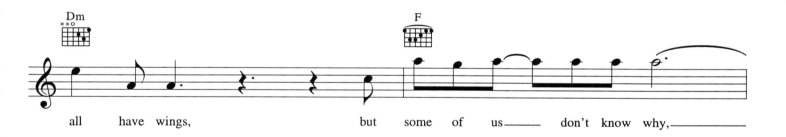

all have wings, but some of us don't know why,

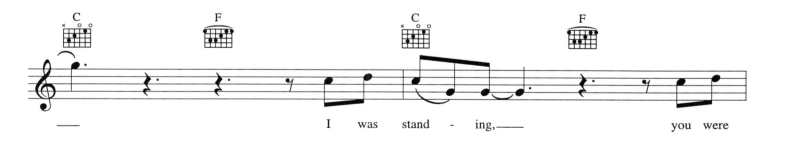

   I was stand - ing,   you were

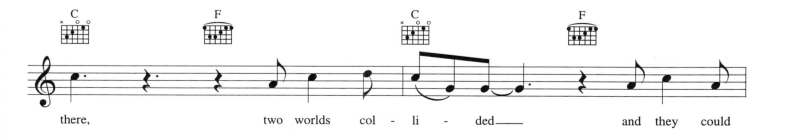

there,   two worlds col - li - ded and they could

OPEN YOUR HEART

Words & Music by Mike Pickering & Paul Heard

© Copyright 1994 EMI Music Publishing Limited, 127 Charing Cross Road, London WC2 (50%)/BMG Music Publishing Limited, 69-79 Fulham High Street, London SW6 (50%).
All Rights Reserved. International Copyright Secured.

(Instrumental)

1. If I on-

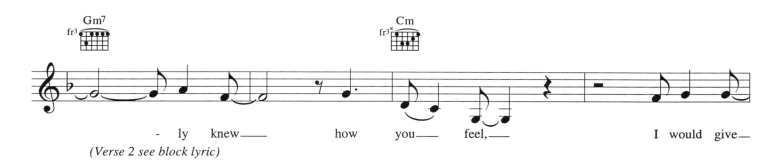

- ly knew___ how you___ feel,___ I would give___

(Verse 2 see block lyric)

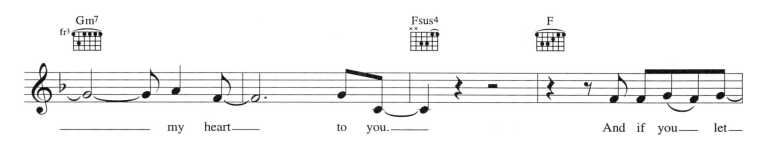

___ my heart___ to you.___ And if you___ let___

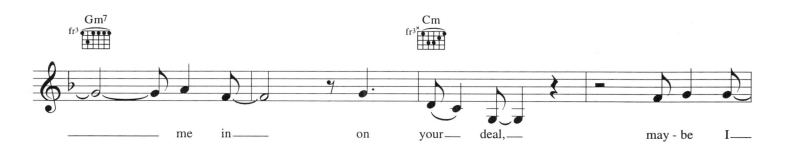

___ me in___ on your___ deal,___ may-be I___

won't feel so blue. Give me a
signal from the heart, some kind of
sign, boy, of who you really are. Don't waste my time 'cause we've come
too far, you must decide now if I'm your star.
O - pen up your heart, o - pen up your heart,
make me feel a part, o - pen up your heart.

To Coda

(Instrumental)

Play 8 times

O - pen up your heart,—

o - pen up your heart.—

Give me a

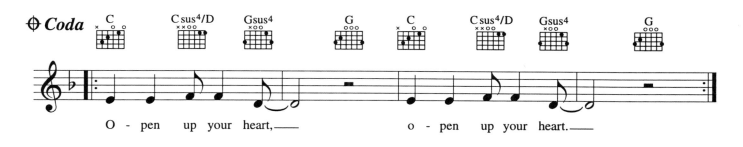

O - pen up your heart,— o - pen up your heart.—

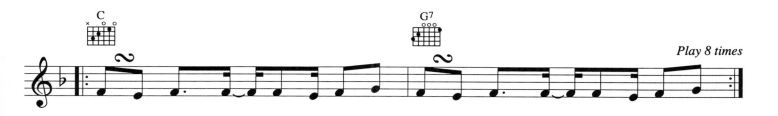

Play 8 times

N.C.

Play 4 times

Verse 2:
Why don't you wear your heart on my sleeve,
Then you can take your place by me.
And I've got more to give than you need,
Come on and end this misery.
Give me a signal from the heart,
Some kind of sign, boy, of who you really are.
Don't waste my time now, we've come too far,
It makes no sense now when we're apart.

ORIGINAL SIN

Words & Music by Andrew Farriss & Michael Hutchence

© Copyright 1983 Browning Music administered by MCA Music Publishing Incorporated, USA for the World.
MCA Music Limited, 77 Fulham Palace Road, London W6.
All Rights Reserved. International Copyright Secured.

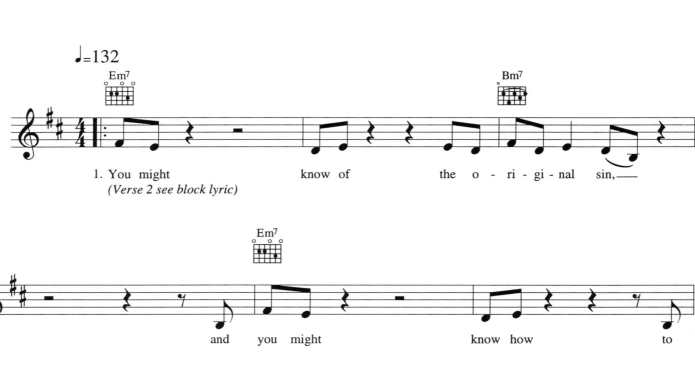

1. You might know of the o - ri - gi - nal sin,
(Verse 2 see block lyric)

and you might know how to

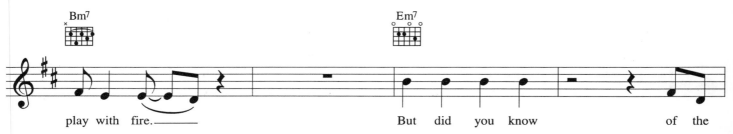

play with fire. But did you know of the

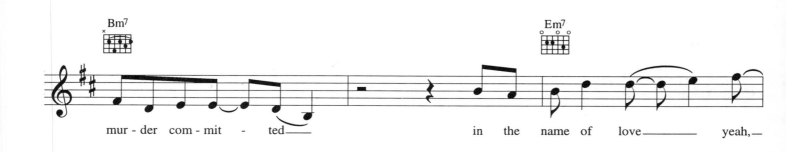

mur - der com - mit - ted in the name of love yeah,

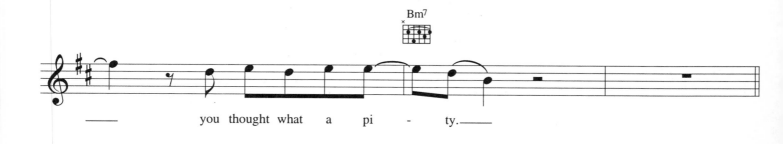

you thought what a pi - ty.

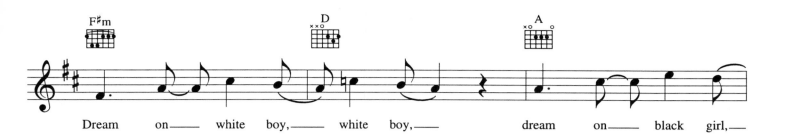

Dream on —— white boy, —— white boy, —— dream on black girl, ——

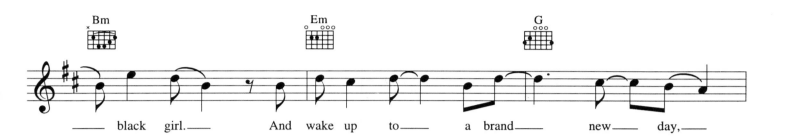

—— black girl. —— And wake up to —— a brand —— new —— day, ——

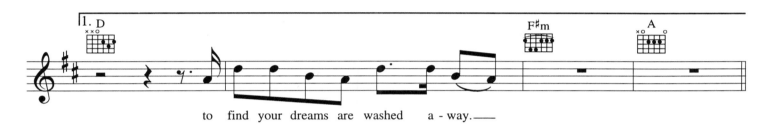

to find your dreams are washed a - way. ——

(Instrumental)

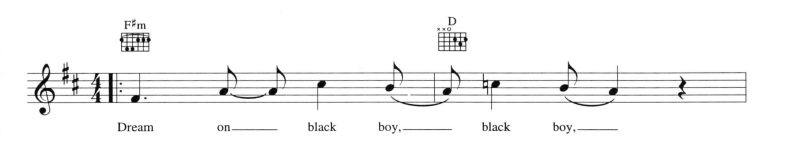

Dream on —— black boy, —— black boy, ——

dream on —— white girl, —— white girl. —— And wake up to —— a brand—

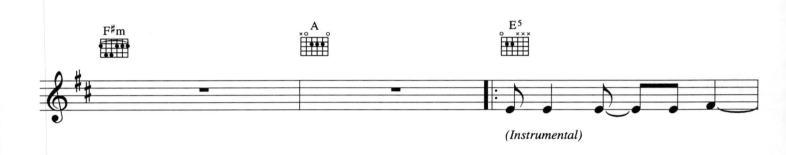

—— new —— day, —— to find your dreams are washed a - way. ——

(Instrumental)

(Vocals ad lib.)

Repeat to fade

Verse 2:
There was a time when I did not care,
And there was a time when the facts did stare.
There is a dream and it's held by many,
Well I'm sure you had to see its open arms.

Dream on white boy, white boy,
Dream on black girl, black girl.
And wake up to a brand new day.

PASS THE DUTCHIE

Words & Music by Jackie Mittoo, Lloyd Ferguson & Fitzroy Simpson

© Copyright 1967 Jackie Mittoo Music. Assigned 1982 to Sparta Florida Music Group Limited, 8/9 Frith Street, London W1.
All Rights Reserved. International Copyright Secured.

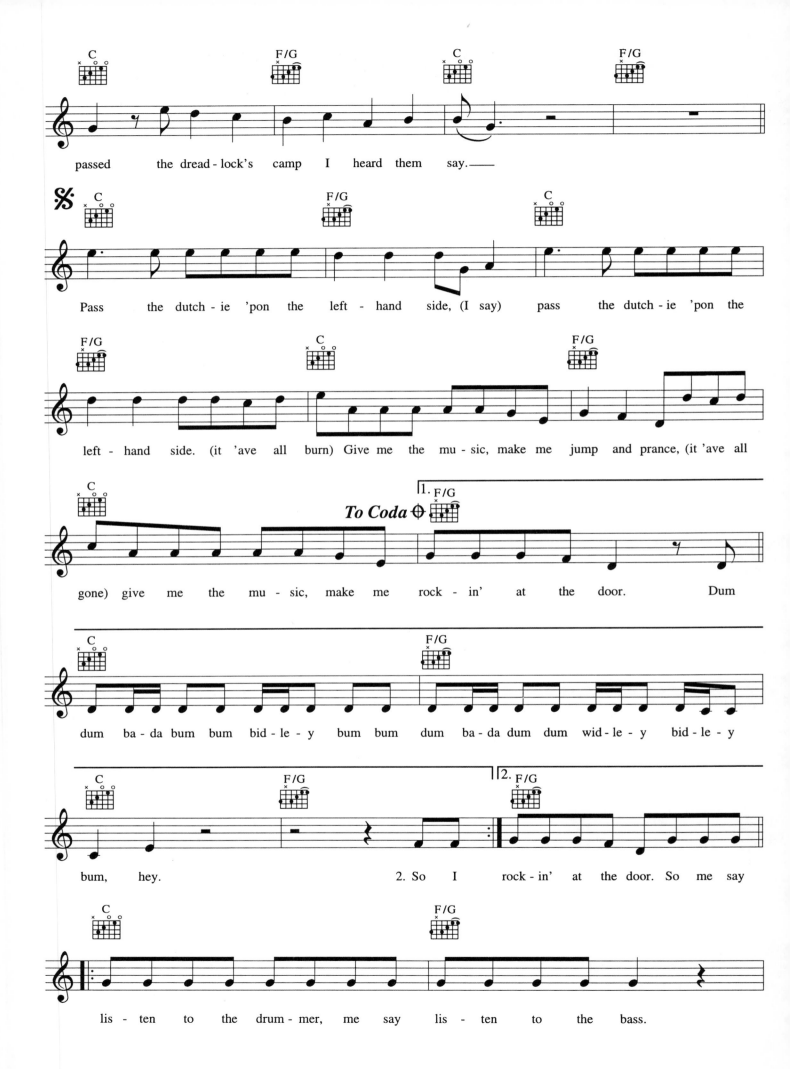

passed   the dread - lock's   camp   I   heard   them   say.——

Pass   the dutch - ie 'pon the   left - hand   side, (I say)   pass   the dutch - ie 'pon the

left - hand   side. (it 'ave all   burn) Give me   the   mu - sic, make me   jump   and prance, (it 'ave all

To Coda ⊕

gone) give   me   the   mu - sic, make me   rock - in'   at   the   door.   Dum

dum ba - da bum bum bid - le - y   bum bum   dum ba - da dum dum wid - le - y   bid - le - y

bum,   hey.   2. So   I   rock - in'   at   the door. So   me say

lis - ten   to   the drum - mer, me say   lis - ten   to   the   bass.

Spoken Intro:

This generation rules the nation with version.
Music happen to be the food of love,
Sounds to really make you rub and scrub.
Dam ba-dam bang ling bidley bong didley bum
Dong bidley bidley bidley bidley bidley bidley bum.
I say:

Verse 2:

So I stopped to find out what was going on,
'Cause the spirit of Jah you know He leads you on.
There was a ring of dreads and the session was there in swing,
And you could feel a chill as I seen and heard them say:

PARKLIFE

Words & Music by Damon Albarn, Graham Coxon, Alex James & David Rowntree

© Copyright 1994 MCA Music Limited, 77 Fulham Palace Road, London W6.
All Rights Reserved. International Copyright Secured.

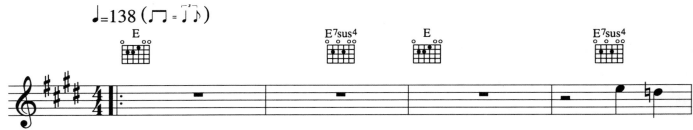

1. *(Spoken)* Confidence is a preference for the habitual voyeur of what is known as park - life.
(Verse 2 see block lyric)

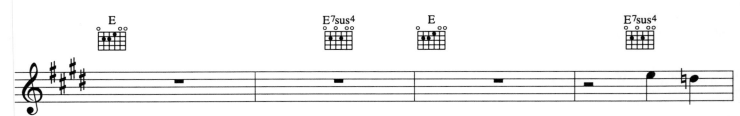

And morning soup can be avoided if you take a route straight through what is known as park - life.

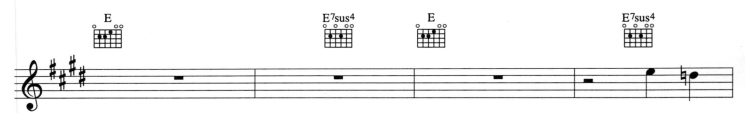

John's got a brewer's droop, he gets intimidated by the dirty pigeons; they love a bit of it, park - life.

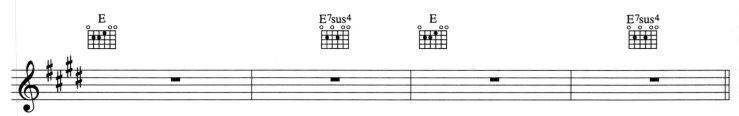

Who's that gut lord marching; you should cut down on your porklife mate, get some exercise.

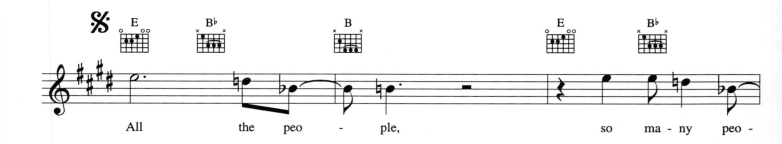

All   the   peo - ple,   so ma - ny peo -

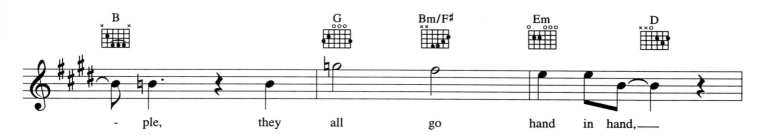

- ple, they all go hand in hand,——

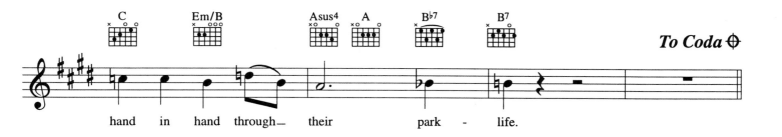

To Coda ✛

hand in hand through— their park - life.

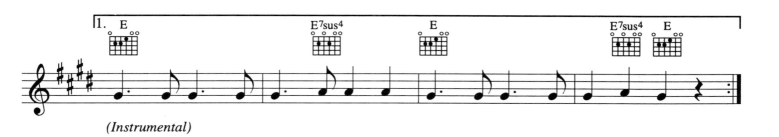

(Instrumental)

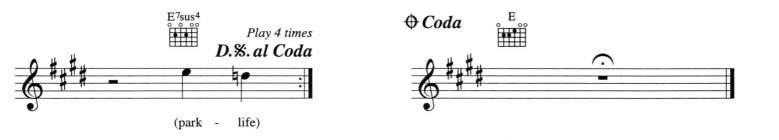

(Spoken 3 & 4) ⎰ It's got nothing to do with your vorsprung durch technic, you know, (park - life)
⎱ and it's not about you joggers who go round and round and round.

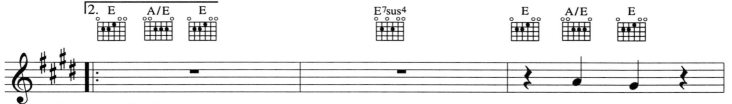

Play 4 times
D.%. al Coda

✛ *Coda*

(park - life)

Verse 2:
I get up when I want except on Wednesday when I get rudely awakened by the dustmen - (park-life)
I put my trousers on, have a cup of tea and I think about leaving the house - (park-life)
I feed the pigeons, I sometimes feed the sparrows too. It gives me a sense of enormous well-being - (park-life)
And then I'm happy for the rest of the day safe in the knowledge there will always be a bit of my heart devoted to it.

ROLL WITH IT

Words & Music by Noel Gallagher

© Copyright 1995 Oasis Music Limited.
Creation Songs/Sony Music Publishing, 10 Great Marlborough Street, London W1.
All Rights Reserved. International Copyright Secured.

♩=130

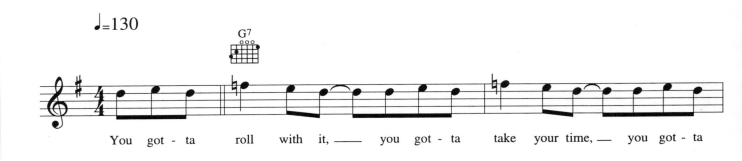

You got-ta roll with it, ___ you got-ta take your time, ___ you got-ta

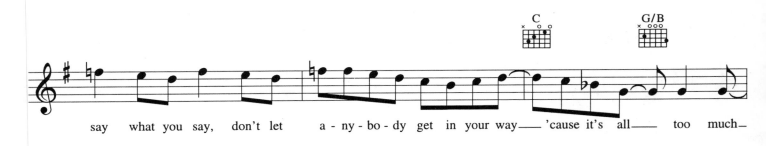

say what you say, don't let a-ny-bo-dy get in your way ___ 'cause it's all ___ too much ___

say what you say, don't let a-ny-bo-dy get in your way ___ 'cause it's all ___ too much ___ for me to take. ___ Don't ev-er

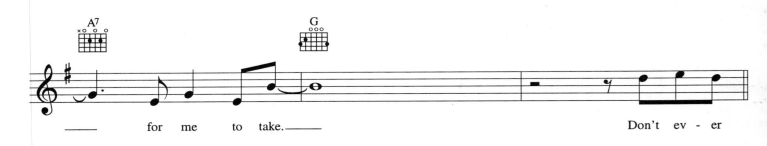

___ for me to take. ___ Don't ev-er

stand a-side, ___ don't ev-er be de-nied, ___ if you wan-na be who you'd be if you're
(*D.%. instrumental*)

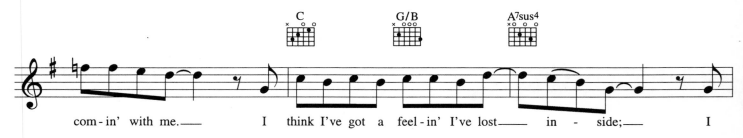

com-in' with me. ___ I think I've got a feel-in' I've lost ___ in-side; ___ I

think I'm gon - na take me a - way____ and____ hide.____ I'm think - ing of things____ that I____

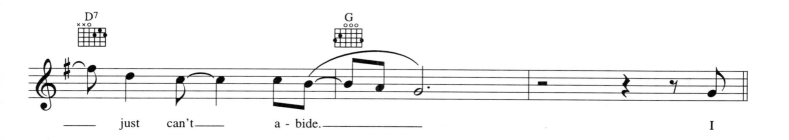

____ just can't____ a - bide._____ I

know the roads____ down which____ your life____ will drive.____ I
(Vocal both times)

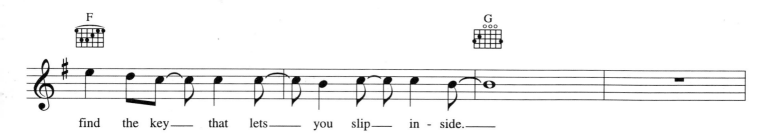

find the key____ that lets____ you slip____ in - side.____

Kiss the girl,____ she's not____ be - hind____ the door._____ You

know, I think I re - cog - nise____ your face,____ but I've ne - ver seen you be - fore.____

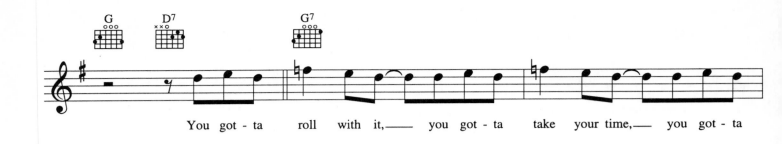

You got - ta   roll   with it,___   you got - ta   take   your time,___   you got - ta

say   what you say,   don't let   a - ny - bo - dy   get   in your way___   'cause it's all___   too   much___

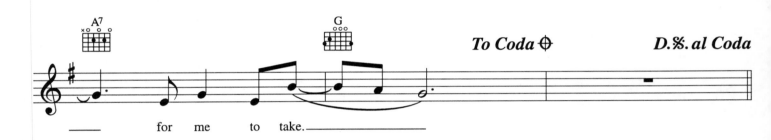

To Coda ⊕   *D.%. al Coda*

___   for   me   to   take.___

⊕ *Coda*

Don't ev - er   stand   a - side,___   don't ev - er   be   de - nied,___   if you wan - na

be   who   you'd   be   if   you're   com - in'   with   me.___   I

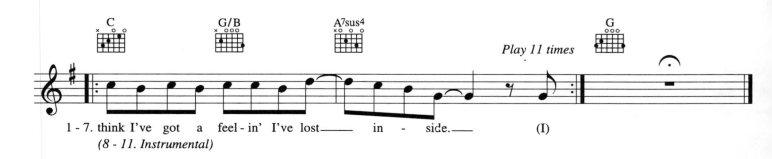

Play 11 times

1 - 7. think I've   got   a   feel - in'   I've lost___   in - side.___   (I)
(8 - 11. Instrumental)

SO GOOD

Words & Music by Martin Brannigan, Stephen Gately, Ronan Keating, Michael Graham, Shane Lynch, Keith Duffy & Roy Hedges

© Copyright 1995 PolyGram Music Publishing Limited, 47 British Grove, London W4 (25%), Island Music Limited, 47 British Grove, London W4 (50%)
& 19 Music/BMG Music Publishing Limited, 69-79 Fulham High Street, London SW6 (25%).
All Rights Reserved. International Copyright Secured.

♩ =106

We're gon-na be so good,——— like on-ly we could,- ——— come on and help——— me now.—— Gon-na be so good,—— like I knew we should.———

1. I've heard it be-fore,—— oh yeah, and you're tel-ling me—— no,—
(Verse 2 see block lyric)

——— and I'm cra - zy. We're talk-ing too fast,——— we've just got-ta

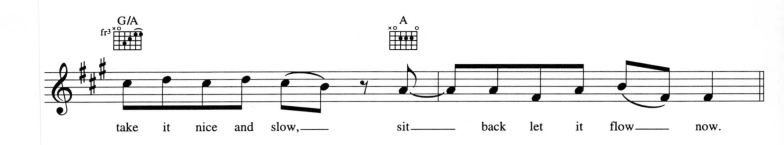

take it nice and slow,_____ sit_____ back let it flow_____ now.

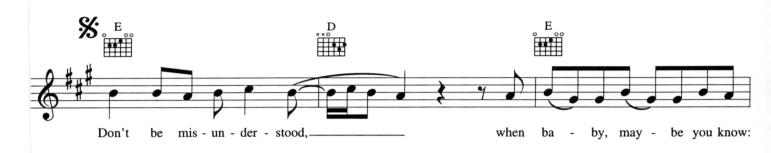

Don't be mis-un-der-stood,_____ _____ when ba-by, may-be you know:

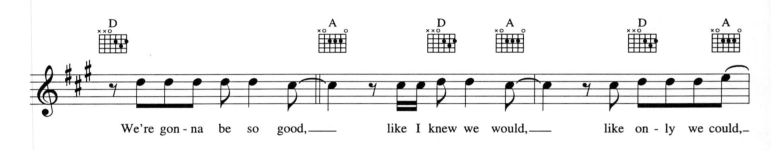

We're gon-na be so good,_____ like I knew we would,_____ like on-ly we could,_

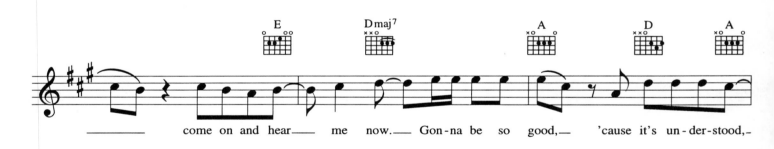

_____ come on and hear_____ me now._____ Gon-na be so good,_____ 'cause it's un-der-stood,_

To Coda ⊕

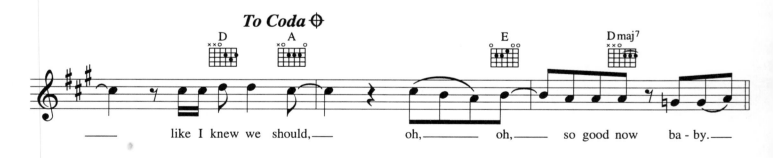

_____ like I knew we should,_____ oh,_____ oh,_____ so good now ba-by._____

We're gon-na be so good,_____

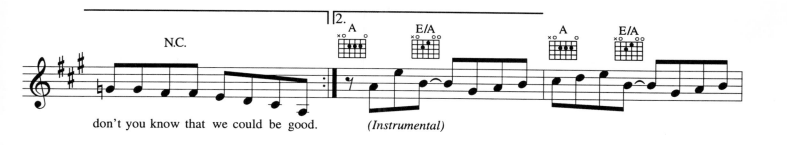

don't you know that we could be good. (Instrumental)

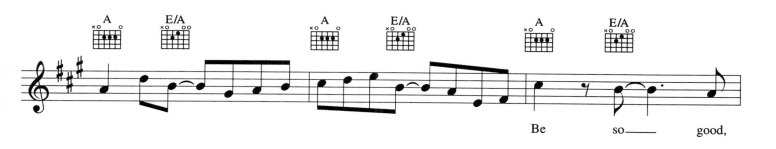

Be so_____ good,

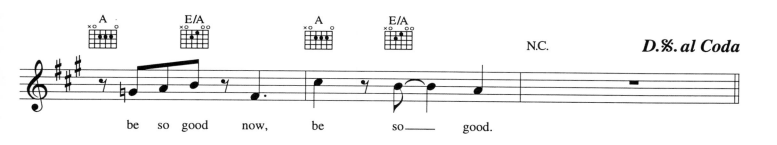

be so good now, be so_____ good.

_____ oh,_____ oh,_____ we're gon-na be so good,_____ like I knew we would,_____

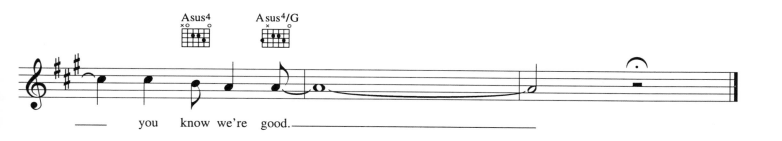

_____ you know we're good._____

Verse 2:
No matter the cost,
When we're out on the town getting lazy.
I'll show you who's boss,
We're just gonna take it all the way,
No matter what they say now.

SINCE I DON'T HAVE YOU

Words by James Beaumont, Janet Vogel & Joseph Verscharen
Music by Walter Lester, John Taylor, Lennie Martin & J Rock

© Copyright 1958 Bonnyview Music Corporation, USA.
Peermusic (UK) Limited, 8-14 Verulam Street, London WC1.
All Rights Reserved. International Copyright Secured.

Verse 2:

And I don't have fond desires,
And I don't have happy hours.
I don't have anything
Since I don't have you.

Verse 3:

I don't have love to share,
And I don't have one who cares.
I don't have anything
Since I don't have you.

STANLEY ROAD

Words & Music by Paul Weller

© Copyright 1995 Stylist Music Limited/BMG Music Publishing Limited, 69-79 Fulham High Street, London SW6.
This Arrangement © Copyright 1996 BMG Music Publishing Limited.
All Rights Reserved. International Copyright Secured.

1. A ha-zy mist hung down— the street,　　the length of its mile—
(Verse 2 see block lyric)

—— as far— as my eye— could see.————————— *(Instrumental)*

The sky so wide, the hous-

-es tall,　　or so they seemed to be,—— so they seemed— to be—

—— so small.——————— *(Instrumental)*

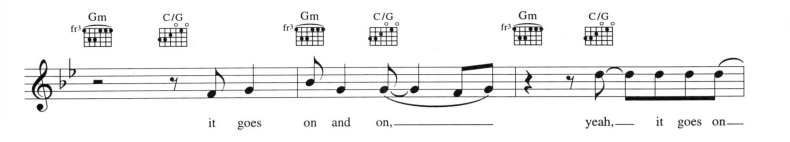

it goes on and on,———— yeah,—— it goes on—

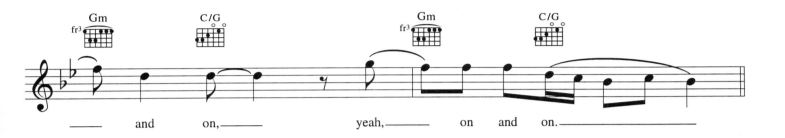

———— and on,———— yeah,———— on and on.————————

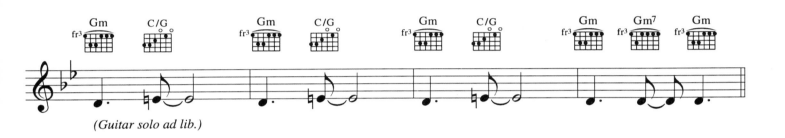

(Guitar solo ad lib.)

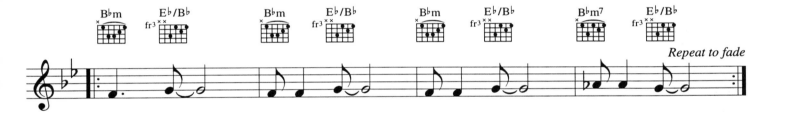

Repeat to fade

Verse 2:
The summer nights that seemed so long
Always call me back to return
As I re-write this song.
The ghosts of night, the dreams of day
Make me swirl and fall and hold me
In their sway.

And it's still in the distance
And it shines like the sun,
Like silver and gold.
It goes on and on,
It goes on and on,
It goes on and on,
It goes on and on.

STAY ANOTHER DAY

Words & Music by Mortimer, Kean & Hawken

© Copyright 1994 Porky Publishing/PolyGram Music Publishing Limited, 47 British Grove, London W4.
All Rights Reserved. International Copyright Secured.

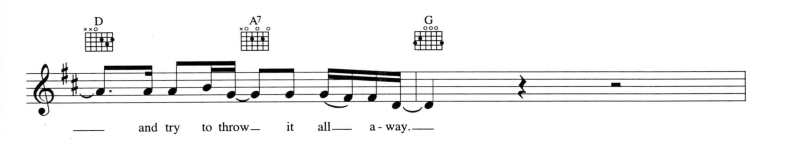

and try to throw— it all— a - way.—

Thought I heard— you say— you love— me, that your love—

was gon - na be— here— to stay.—

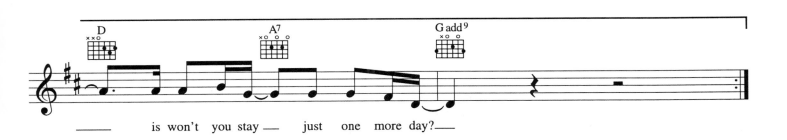

I've on - ly just be - gun— to know— you, all I can say—

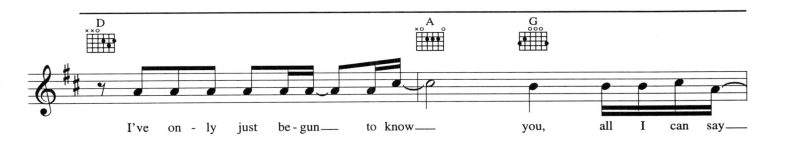

is won't you stay — just one more day?—

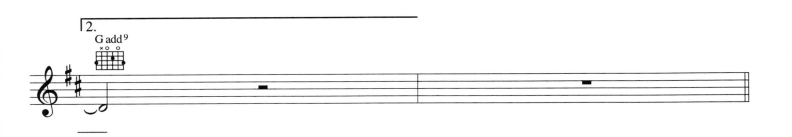

Ba - by if you've got to go—— a - way,—— don't think I can take the pain,—

—— won't you stay an - oth - er day?——

Oh don't leave me a - lone—— like this,—— don't you say it's the fi - nal kiss,—

Play 3 times   *Repeat to fade*

—— won't you stay an - oth - er day?——

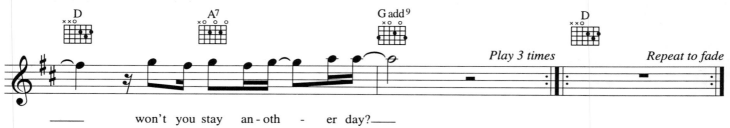

Verse 2:
I touch your face while you are sleeping
And hold your hand,
Don't understand what's going on.
Good times we had return to haunt me,
Though it's for you,
All that I do seems to be wrong.

STEREOTYPES

Words & Music by Damon Albarn, Graham Coxon, Alex James & David Rowntree

© Copyright 1995 MCA Music Limited, 77 Fulham Palace Road, London W6.
All Rights Reserved. International Copyright Secured.

time to time you know you should be go - ing on an - oth - er bend - er.

(Instrumental)

2. The

To Coda ⊕

Yes,_____ there must be more to life than ste - re - o -

types. (Guitar solo)

Wife

swap - ping is the fut - ure, you know that it would suit you.

Coda

types. All your life you're dream - ing,_____ and then you

stop dream - ing, from time to time you know you

should go on an - oth - er bend - er, be - fore you come to an end - er._____

Verse 2:

The suburbs they are sleeping
But he's dressing up tonight.
She likes a man in uniform, he loves to wear it tight.
They are on the lover's sofa, they are on the patio,
And when the fun is over watch themselves on video.

The neighbours may be staring
But they are just past caring.

STILL LIFE

Words & Music by Brett Anderson & Bernard Butler

© Copyright 1994 PolyGram Music Publishing Limited, 47 British Grove, London W4.
All Rights Reserved. International Copyright Secured.

still,_____ still_____ life.

(Instrumental)

Repeat to fade

Verse 2:

Is this still life all I'm good for too?
There by the window quietly killed for you,
And they drive by like insects do,
They think they don't know me,
They hired a car for you.
To go into the night, into the night,
She and I into the night.

SUPERSONIC

Words & Music by Noel Gallagher

© Copyright 1994 Oasis Music Limited.
Creation Songs Limited/Sony Music Publishing, 10 Great Marlborough Street, London W1.
All Rights Reserved. International Copyright Secured.

-low sub-ma-rine. You need to find out,___ 'cause no-one's gon-na tell {you her} what I'm

on a-bout. You need to find a way___ for what___

___ you want to say, but be-fore___ to-mor-row, 'cause

my friend said___ he'd take___ you home,___ he sits in a cor-ner all___

___ a-lone.___ He lives un-der a wa-ter-fall,___

no-bo-dy can see him, no-bo-dy can ev-er hear him call, no-

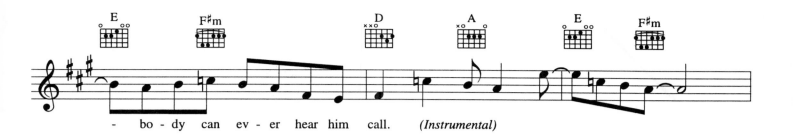

- bo - dy can ev - er hear him call. *(Instrumental)*

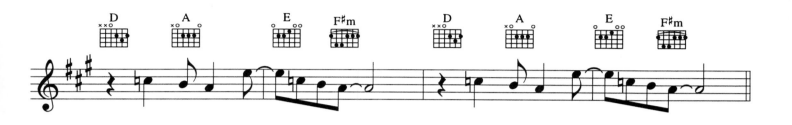

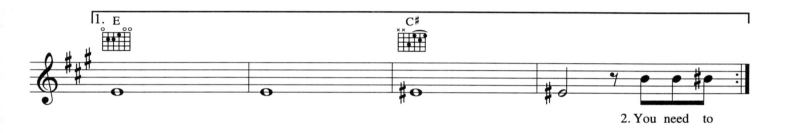

2. You need to

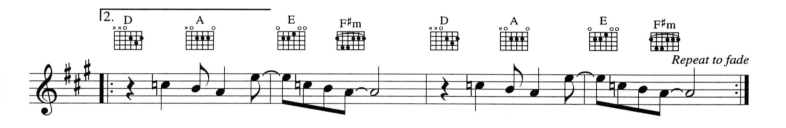

Repeat to fade

Verse 2:

You need to be yourself,
You can't be no one else.
I know a girl called Elsa,
She's into Alka Seltzer
She sniffs it through a cane
On a supersonic train.

And he makes me laugh,
I got her autograph.
She done it with a doctor
On a helicopter,
She's sniffing in her tissue
Selling the Big Issue.

And she finds out...

TEARS IN HEAVEN

Words & Music by Eric Clapton & Will Jennings

© Copyright 1991 & 1996 E. C. Music Limited, London NW1 (87.5%).
© Copyright 1991 Blue Sky Rider Songs administered by Rondor Music (London) Limited, 10a Parsons Green, London SW6 for the World (excluding USA & Canada) (12.5%).
All Rights Reserved. International Copyright Secured.

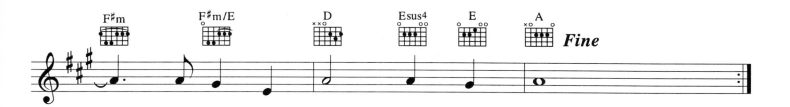

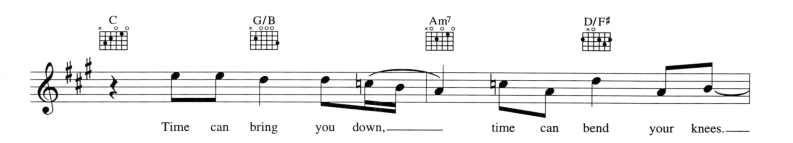

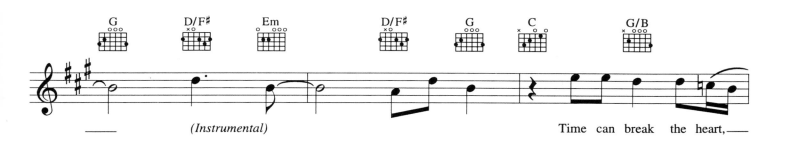

Time can bring you down,———— time can bend your knees.——

—— (Instrumental) Time can break the heart,——

D.C. al Fine

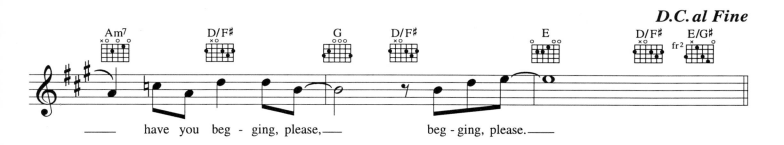

—— have you beg - ging, please,—— beg - ging, please.——

Verse 2:

Would you hold my hand
If I saw you in heaven?
Would you help me stand
If I saw you in heaven?
I'll find my way
Through night and day,
'Cause I know I just can't stay
Here in heaven.

Verse 3: (D.S.)

Instrumental solo - 8 bars

Beyond the door
There's peace I'm sure;
And I know there'll be no more
Tears in heaven.

Verse 4: (D.%.)

Would you know my name
If I saw you in heaven?
Would you be the same
If I saw you in heaven?
I must be strong and carry on,
'Cause I know I don't belong
Here in heaven.

THE SIGN

Words & Music by Buddha, Joker, Jenny & Linn

© Copyright 1992 Megasong Publishing, Sweden.
PolyGram Music Publishing Limited, 47 British Grove, London W4.
All Rights Reserved. International Copyright Secured.

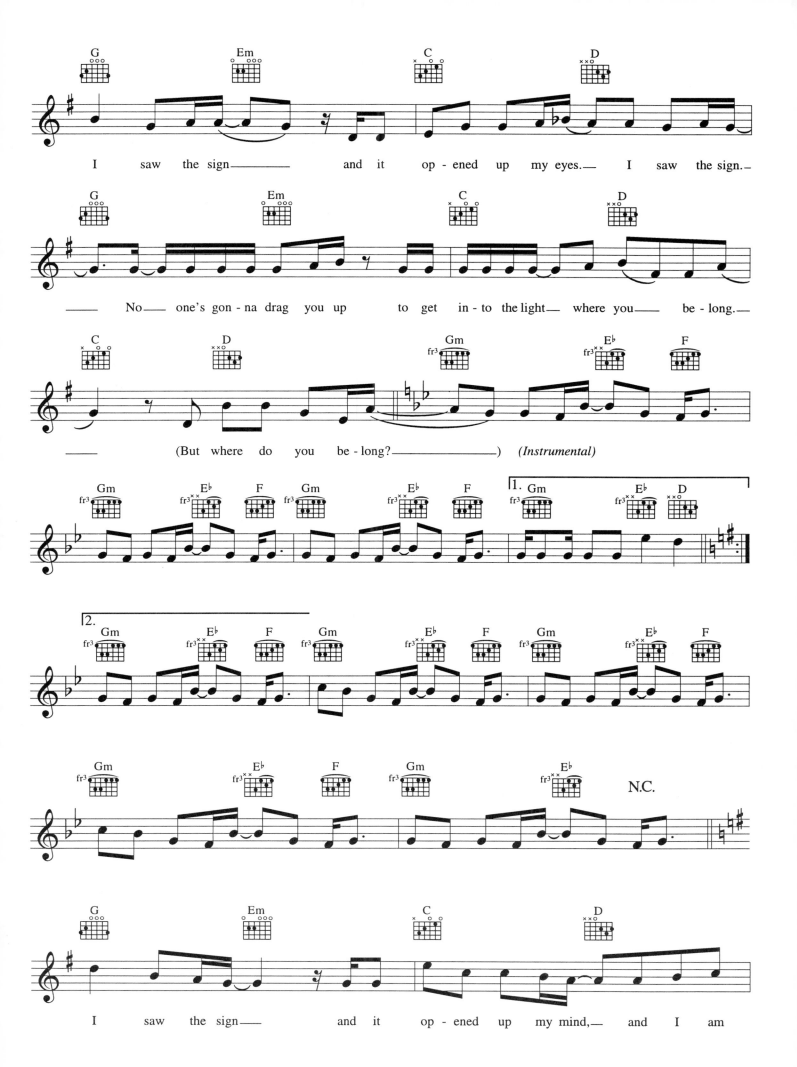

I saw the sign_____ and it op-ened up my eyes.___ I saw the sign.__

_____ No___ one's gon-na drag you up to get in-to the light__ where you___ be-long.__

_____ (But where do you be-long?_____) (Instrumental)

I saw the sign___ and it op-ened up my mind,___ and I am

Verse 2:
Under the pale moon,
For so many years I wondered who you are.
How could a person like you bring me joy
Under the pale moon, where I see a lot of stars?
Is enough enough?

THE UNIVERSAL

Words & Music by Damon Albarn, Graham Coxon, Alex James & David Rowntree

© Copyright 1995 MCA Music Limited, 77 Fulham Palace Road, London W6.
All Rights Reserved. International Copyright Secured.

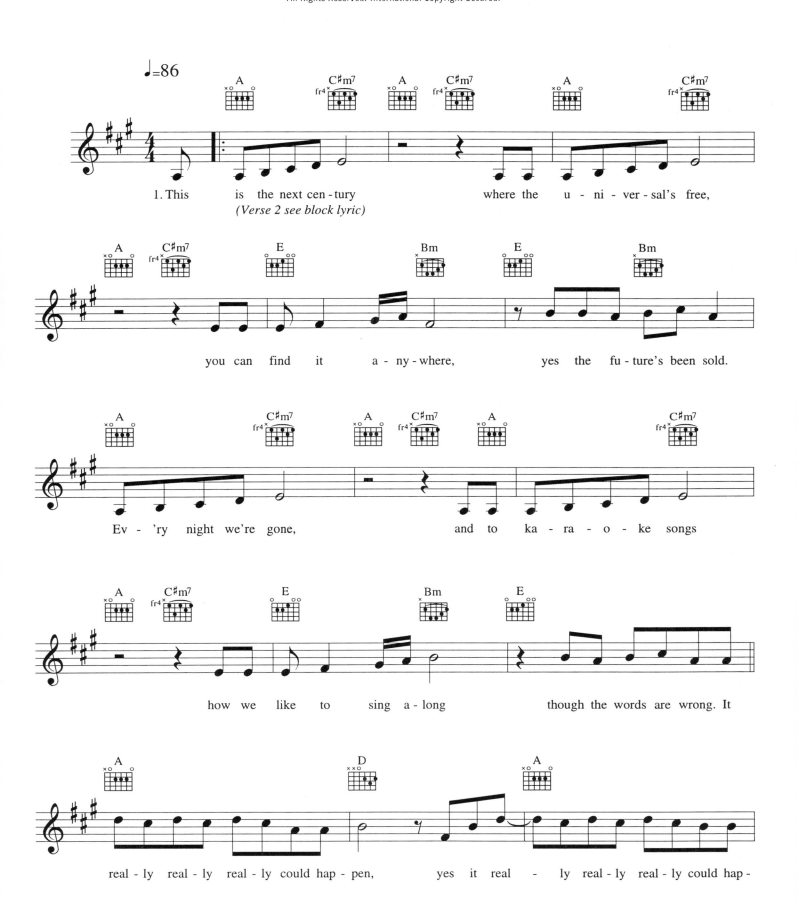

1. This is the next cen - tury where the u - ni - ver - sal's free,

(Verse 2 see block lyric)

you can find it a - ny - where, yes the fu - ture's been sold.

Ev - 'ry night we're gone, and to ka - ra - o - ke songs

how we like to sing a - long though the words are wrong. It

real - ly real - ly real - ly could hap - pen, yes it real - ly real - ly real - ly could hap -

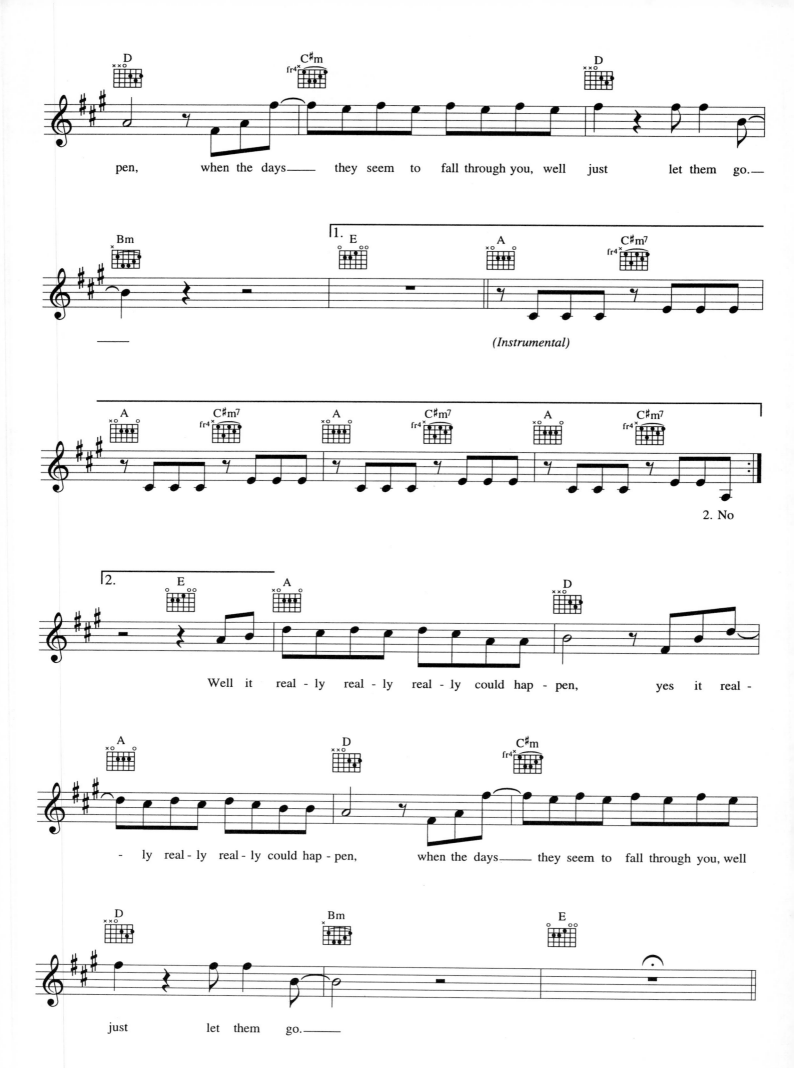

pen,   when the days——— they seem to fall through you, well just   let them go.——

——

(Instrumental)

2. No

Well it real - ly real - ly real - ly could hap - pen,   yes it real -

- ly real - ly real - ly could hap - pen,   when the days——— they seem to fall through you, well

just   let them go.———

(Instrumental)

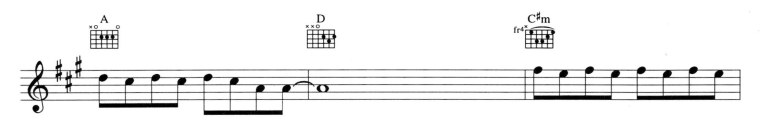

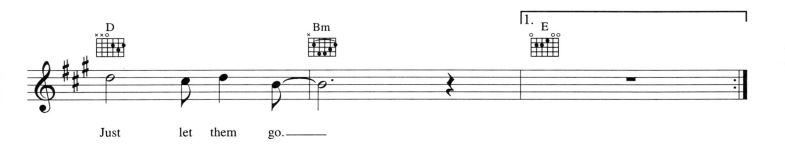

Just   let   them   go.————

rall.

Verse 2:
No one here is alone,
Satellites in every home,
The universal's here,
Here for everyone.

Every paper that you read
Says tomorrow's your lucky day,
Well, here's your lucky day.

TO THE END

Words & Music by Damon Albarn, Graham Coxon, Alex James & David Rowntree

© Copyright 1994 MCA Music Limited, 77 Fulham Palace Road, London W6.
All Rights Reserved. International Copyright Secured.

Verse 2:

What happened to us,
Soon it will be gone forever,
Infatuated only with ourselves,
And neither of us can think straight anymore.

THIS AIN'T A LOVE SONG

Words & Music by Jon Bon Jovi, Richie Sambora & Desmond Child

© Copyright 1995 Bon Jovi Publishing/PolyGram International Publishing Incorporated, Aggressive Music & EMI April Music Incorporated/Desmobile Music Company Incorporated, USA.
PolyGram Music Publishing Limited, 47 British Grove, London W4 (66.66%)/EMI Songs Limited, 127 Charing Cross Road, London WC2 (33.33%).
All Rights Reserved. International Copyright Secured.

1. I should-'ve seen it com-ing when the ros-es died,

(Verse 2 see block lyric)

should-'ve seen the end of sum-mer in your eyes,

I should-'ve lis-tened when you said good-night,— you real-ly—— meant good-bye.—

Ba-by ain't it fun-ny how you ne-ver ev-er learn to fall,———

you're real-ly on your knees when you think you're stand-ing tall,

but on-ly fools are know-it-alls,____ and I played that___ fool for you. I

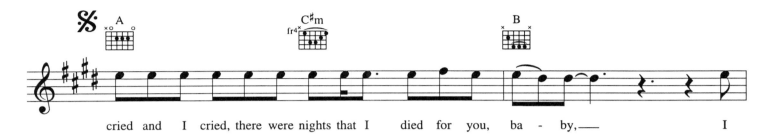

cried and I cried, there were nights that I died for you, ba - by,___ I

tried and I tried to de - ny your love drove me cra - zy, ba - by, if the

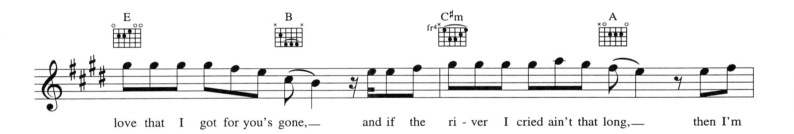

love that I got for you's gone,___ and if the ri - ver I cried ain't that long,___ then I'm

wrong, yeah I'm wrong,_ this ain't a love song._____ love song.___ If the

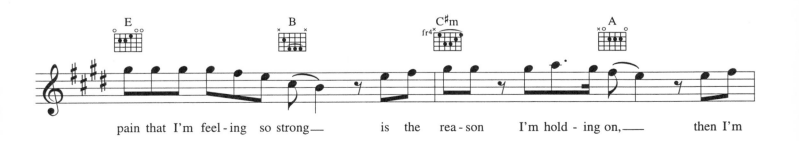

pain that I'm feel-ing so strong___ is the rea - son I'm hold-ing on,___ then I'm

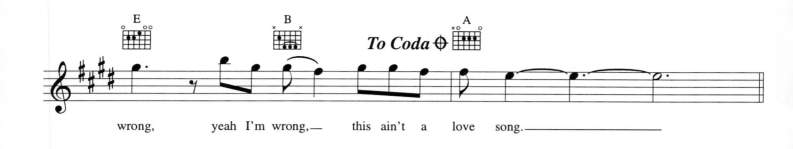

wrong,   yeah I'm wrong,—   this ain't a   love   song.————————

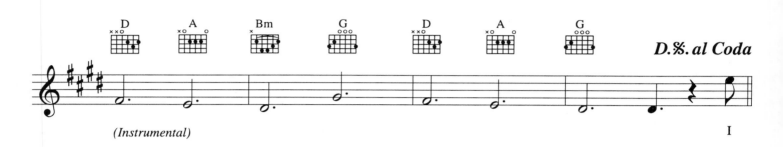

(Instrumental)   I

love   song.——   Then I'm   wrong,   yeah I'm wrong,—   this ain't a

love   song.——   Then I'm   wrong, yeah I'm wrong,–   this ain't a   love song.————

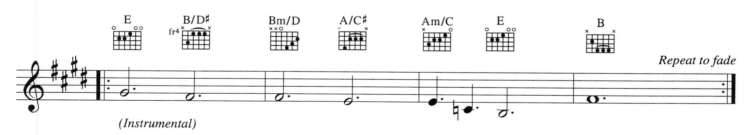

(Instrumental)

Verse 2:
Baby, I thought you and me would stand the test of time,
Like we got away with the perfect crime.
But we were just a legend in my mind,
I guess that I was blind.
Remember those nights dancing at the masquerade?
The clowns wore smiles that wouldn't fade.
You and I were renegades,
Some things never change.

It made me so mad 'cause I wanted it bad for us, baby,
And now it's so sad that whatever we had ain't worth saving.

WE ARE THE PIGS

Words & Music by Brett Anderson & Bernard Butler

© Copyright 1994 PolyGram Music Publishing Limited, 47 British Grove, London W4.
All Rights Reserved. International Copyright Secured.

♩=108

1. Well the church bells are cal - ling, po -
(Verse 2 see block lyric)

lice cars on fire_____ and as they call you to the eye of the storm—

_____ all the peo - ple say "Stay at home___ to - night".___ I say

we are___ the pigs, ___ we are___ the swine,—

1. we are___ the stars___ of the fire_____ of the fir - ing line.—

_____ *(Instrumental)* 2. And as the

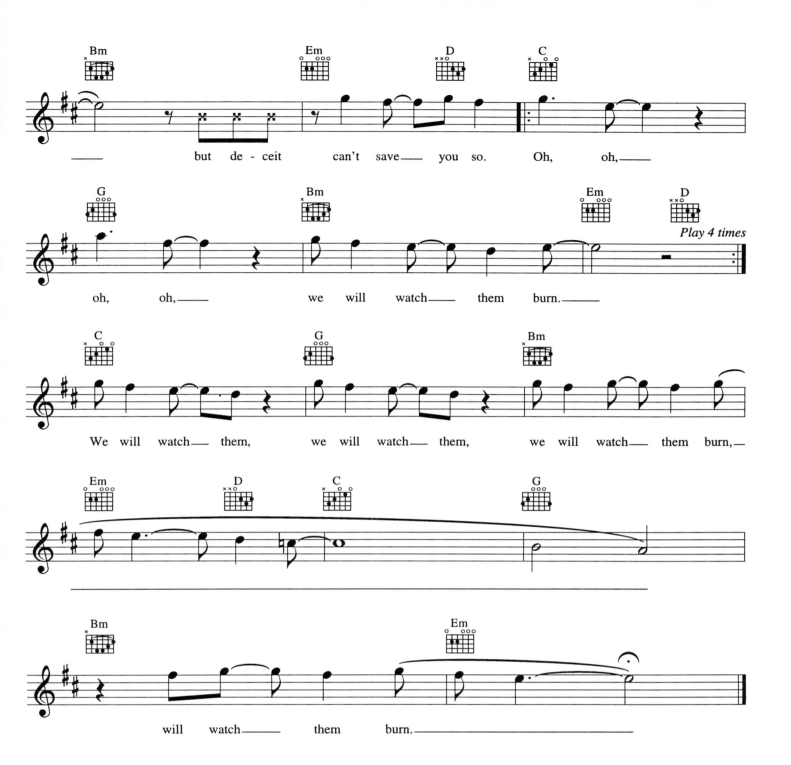

Verse 2:
And as the smack cracks at your window,
You wake up with a gun in your mouth,
Oh, let the nuclear wind blow away my sins
And I'll stay at home in my house.

WILD WOOD

Words & Music by Paul Weller

© Copyright 1993 Notting Hill Music (UK) Limited.
All Rights Reserved. International Copyright Secured.

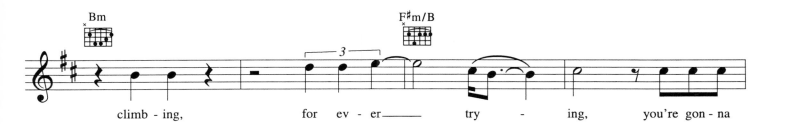

climb - ing, for ev - er____ try - ing, you're gon - na

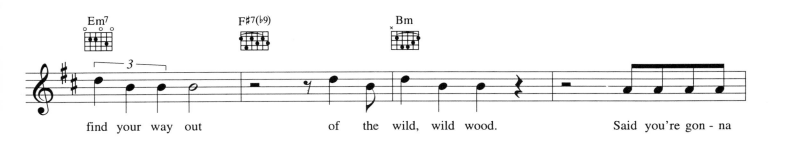

find your way out of the wild, wild wood. Said you're gon - na

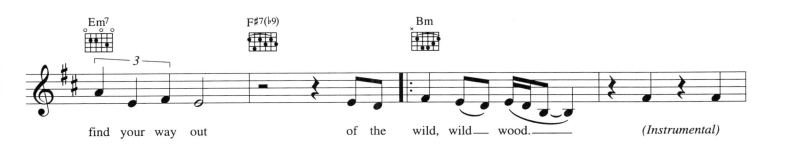

find your way out of the wild, wild____ wood.____ *(Instrumental)*

Verse 2:

Don't let them get you down,
Making you feel guilty about
Golden rain will bring you riches,
All the good things you deserve now.

Verse 3:

Climbing, forever trying,
Find your way out of the wild, wild wood.
Now there's no justice,
You've only yourself that you can trust in.

Verse 4:

And I said high tide, mid-afternoon,
People fly by in the traffic's boom.
Knowing just where you're blowing,
Getting to where you should be going.

Verse 5:

Day by day your world fades away,
Waiting to feel all the dreams that say,
Golden rain will bring you riches,
All the good things you deserve now.

YOU DO SOMETHING TO ME

Words & Music by Paul Weller

© Copyright 1995 Stylist Music Limited/BMG Music Publishing Limited, 69-79 Fulham High Street, London SW6.
This Arrangement © Copyright 1996 BMG Music Publishing Limited.
All Rights Reserved. International Copyright Secured.

Verse 4:
You do something to me, somewhere deep inside.
I'm hoping to get close to a peace I cannot find.

Verse 5:
Dancing through the fire, yeah, just to catch a flame.
Just to get close to, just close enough to tell you that:

YOU GIVE LOVE A BAD NAME

Words & Music by Jon Bon Jovi, Richie Sambora & Desmond Child

© Copyright 1986 Bon Jovi Publishing/EMI April Music Incorporated/Desmobile Music Company Incorporated/PolyGram Music Publishing Incorporated, USA.
PolyGram Music Publishing Limited, 47 British Grove, London W4 (66.66%)/EMI Songs Limited, 127 Charing Cross Road, London WC2 (33.33%).
All Rights Reserved. International Copyright Secured.

♩=118

N.C.

Shot through the heart—— and you're to—— blame, dar-lin' you give—— love——— a bad name.

(Instrumental)

1. The an-gel's smile—— is
(Verse 2 see block lyric)

what you sell, you pro-mise me hea-ven then put me through hell. The

chains of love—— got a hold on me, when pas-sion's a pri-son, you

can't break—— free. Oh—— you're a load-ed gun,——

Verse 2:
Paint your smile on your lips,
Blood red nails on your fingertips.
A schoolboy's dream, you act so shy,
Your very first kiss was your first kiss goodbye.

ZOMBIE

Words & Music by Dolores O'Riordan

© Copyright 1994 Island Music Limited, 47 British Grove, London W4.
All Rights Reserved. International Copyright Secured.

WHEN LOVE AND HATE COLLIDE

Words & Music by Joe Elliott & Rick Savage

© Copyright 1995 Bludgeon Riffola Limited, administered by Zomba Music Publishers Limited, 165-167 High Road, London NW10 for the World.
All Rights Reserved. International Copyright Secured.

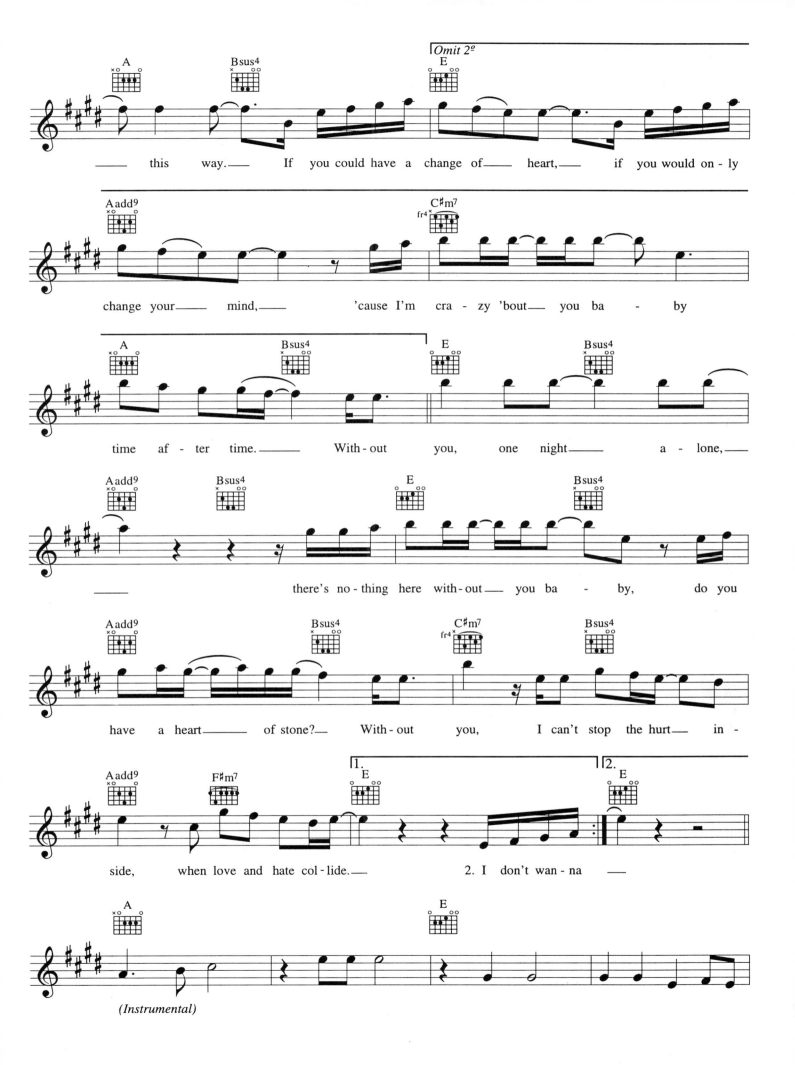

this way.___ If you could have a change of___ heart,___ if you would on-ly

change your___ mind,___ 'cause I'm cra-zy 'bout___ you ba - by

time af-ter time.___ With-out you, one night___ a - lone,___

___ there's no-thing here with-out___ you ba - by, do you

have a heart___ of stone?___ With-out you, I can't stop the hurt___ in-

side, when love and hate col-lide.___ 2. I don't wan-na ___

(Instrumental)

Verse 2:
I don't wanna fight no more,
I don't know what we're fighting for
When we treat each other, baby,
Like an act of war.
I could tell a million lies
And it would come as no surprise,
When the truth is like a stranger,
Hits you right between the eyes.